THE HOME BOOK OF
INDIAN COOKERY

THE HOME BOOK OF
Indian Cookery

Sipra Das Gupta

FABER AND FABER
London · Boston

First published in 1973
by Faber and Faber Limited
3 Queen Square London WC1
First published in Faber Paperbacks 1980
Printed in Great Britain by
Whitstable Litho Ltd, Whitstable
All rights reserved

British Library Cataloguing in Publication Data

Das Gupta, Sipra
   The home book of Indian cookery
   1. Cookery, India
   I. Title
   641.5'954   TX724.5.14

   ISBN 0-571-11508-x

Acknowledgements

It was my husband who first suggested that I should write a cookery book. He and my daughter acted throughout both as critics and connoisseurs of my cooking.

I am grateful to many friends in India and abroad who helped me try out the recipes or shared their own recipes with me. I must mention in particular Manju Chatterjee, Neela Basu, Sunanda Sen and Uma Sambamurty. Tutu Das Gupta, Krishna Pal, Sumita Sen and Letha Woods often participated in my cooking sessions at our Montreal apartment.

Miss Lise Brault typed the whole manuscript efficiently and with much patience. Lastly, I must express my gratitude to Miss Naseem Khan who went through the manuscript imaginatively and prepared it for the press.

Contents

Weights, Measures and Oven Temperatures

Dry Weights and Measures (approx.)

1 kilogram = 1,000 grams = 2 lb. 3 oz.
1 lb. = 16 oz. = 450 grams
1 oz. = 30 grams

grams	oz.		grams	lb./oz
15 =	$\frac{1}{2}$		225 =	8 ($\frac{1}{2}$ lb.)
30 =	1	($\frac{1}{4}$ kilo)	250 =	9
50 =	$1\frac{2}{3}$		450 =	16 (1 lb.)
60 =	2	($\frac{1}{2}$ kilo)	500 =	18
90 =	3		675 =	1 lb. 8 oz.
100 =	$3\frac{1}{2}$	($\frac{3}{4}$ kilo)	750 =	1 lb. 10 oz.
113 =	4		900 =	2 lb.
125 =	$4\frac{1}{3}$		1 kilo =	2 lb. 3 oz.
150 =	$5\frac{1}{3}$		$1\frac{1}{2}$ kilos =	3 lb. 5 oz.
170 =	6		2 kilos =	4 lb. 6 oz.
200 =	7			

Liquid Measurements (approx.)

2 teaspoons = 1 dessertspoon
3 teaspoons = 1 tablespoon
5 tablespoons = $\frac{1}{2}$ cup or $\frac{1}{2}$ wineglass = 3 fluid oz. = 84 ml.
10 tablespoons = 1 cup or 1 wineglass = 6 fluid oz. = 168 ml.

Fluid Ounces into Millilitres (approx.)

Fluid Ounces	Millilitres
1	28
5 ($\frac{1}{4}$ pint)	140
9	252 ($\frac{1}{4}$ litre)
10 ($\frac{1}{2}$ pint)	280
12	336 ($\frac{1}{3}$ litre)
15 ($\frac{3}{4}$ pint)	420
18	504 ($\frac{1}{2}$ litre)
20 (1 pint)	560
35$\frac{3}{4}$	1,000 (1 litre)

Comparative Oven Temperatures

GAS OVEN SETTINGS	ELECTRIC OVEN SETTINGS		
	Fahrenheit	*Centigrade*	
$\frac{1}{4}$	225°	110°	⎫
$\frac{1}{2}$	250°	130°	⎬ Very Slow
1	275°	140°	⎭
2	300°	150°	⎫
3	325°	160°	⎬ Slow
4	350°	180°	Very Moderate
5	375°	190°	Moderate
6	400°	200°	⎫
7	425°	220°	⎬ Moderately Hot
8	450°	230°	Hot
9	475°	240°	Very Hot

I

Introduction

A western friend of mine enjoying his first fully-fledged Indian meal remarked, 'India is such a poor country, but her food is so rich and varied!' But poverty is relatively a modern phenomenon in India while her cuisine is rooted in a prosperous civilization of long antiquity.

Ancient Indian cookery was not basically different from that of the present time. This continuity arises primarily from the fact that the basic ingredients, herbs and spices used today date back to antiquity. For instance, I regard dahi (yoghourt) and ghee (clarified butter) as the two essential ingredients of Indian cooking. Both were mentioned in the *Rig Veda* (around 2000 B.C.). Similarly the Buddhist text, the *Jatakas*, refer to a wide variety of spices, among them garlic, jiraka (cumin seed), pippali (pepper), haridra (turmeric), ardaka (ginger) and kara leaves, all of which still figure prominently in our cooking.

Again, the articles of food cooked date back to antiquity. As early as the pre-Christian Vedic age we find that the food of the common people included basic cereals like rice and wheat and that they had varied preparations of goat-meat, mutton, lamb, venison, etc. Varieties of pulses, oil seeds, green vegetables, sugar candy and molasses came soon after. Not only milk but its various products were known. The *Vinaya* texts emphasize five dairy products: milk, dahi, ghee, buttermilk and butter.

While unchanged in essentials, Indian cuisine assimilated over the centuries traditions and habits of peoples who came to India and made it their home. Like art and architecture, Indian cuisine shows unmistakeable signs of absorbing and assimilating those who came. The Muslims in particular brought their own rich traditions and contributed handsomely to the evolution of Indian cuisine. Moghul courts were well-known patrons of the culinary art, e. g. the well-known medieval text *Ain-I Akbari* includes a section called 'Recipes for Dishes'.

Within the broad pattern set by basic ingredients, herbs and spices, different regions in India evolved their own cuisine. The wide variations in soil and climate in India influence regional products which, in turn, give character to regional cooking. Thus coconut, which is plentiful in the south, is used widely in preparing food there, while it is rarely used in the north-west. Again, types of vegetable oil used in different regions differ depending on the local agricultural pattern.

One of the most important characteristics of Indian cooking is the delicate blending of spices and herbs. Whether one is a good cook or not depends on one's 'touch' with the spices. This probably explains why mothers in Indian homes teach their daughters not by giving them 'exact measurements' but by helping them to cultivate a sense of smell and colour, which show subtle shades depending on the exact proportions of different spices used.

Again, the contrast of opposite tastes is a special characteristic of Indian cooking. Here also we find regional variations. In Bengal, the emphasis is on the contrast between sweet and sour while in Tamilnadu hot and sour tastes are the favourite combination.

Indian meals insist on a balance of richness and simplicity so that food is never too heavy. In day-to-day cooking the emphasis is more on simplicity than on richness. Rich dishes are more for holidays and festive occasions which, of course, occur with unusual frequency in India. The idea that Indian meals consist simply of 'hot and undigestible curries' is a myth which I hope this book will help to dispel.

In serving food in India, I think the emphasis is more on cleanliness than on decoration. Every utensil must be washed in clean water. You may touch food only after you wash your hands. In traditional households, even today, you must take off shoes that have been used out of doors before entering the kitchen or dining-room. Bathing before main meals and washing the mouth and hands after every meal are the traditional habits of all people, rich and poor.

The normal menu in the Indian cuisine consists of a rice or bread variety, a vegetable, a pulse, a meat or fish dish followed by a chutney and a sweet dish. For serving with fish, rice is preferred to bread. When guests are entertained, it is usual to prepare pilau or fried rice rather than plain rice; it is also usual to offer both sweet yoghourt and a sweet made of chhana or khoya. Payes preparations are not taken with yoghourt.

This book is only an introduction to Indian cooking. It is particularly designed for Western kitchens. Indeed, I cooked all these dishes using ingredients and utensils available either in England or in America where I lived for a long time. There I often used to select a spice, herb or vegetable which would serve as a substitute for an Indian ingredient. Sometimes, I found a simple and easily available substitute for some classical ingredient which might require a lot of extra labour. I found that many typical dishes could be prepared in the oven, thereby reducing the amount of attention needed. I have kept these experiences in mind in writing this book.

2

Glossary of Spices

❧

India is a land of spices. From ancient times, India has exported spices to the rest of the world. For instance, Rev. T. Foulker concluded, in the nineteenth century, that, 'with a very high degree of probability some of the most esteemed of the spices which were carried by the Mediantish merchants of Genesis XXXIII 25–28 and by the sons of the Pharoah Jacob (Genesis XLIII.II) had been cultivated in the spice-gardens of the Deccan'. In the later age the export of spices from India played a crucial role in the traditional gold drain from Imperial Rome to India. It is no wonder that spices play a crucial role in Indian cuisine.

Spices used in the recipes

Indian food is essentially a blending of flavours and colours. Varied spices are essential to it.

Turmeric (haldi) is the powdered form (yellow in colour) of a root related to the ginger family. It is the most universally used spice in Indian cookery.

Cumin (zeera) is used in both forms—seeds and powder. Freshly ground cumin has a sharper and more pleasant smell than the prepared ground form.

Coriander (dhania) is used both in seed and powdered form. Green coriander leaves are frequently used to give a delicate aroma. Use only the green leaves and throw away the stems.

Cardamoms (ilaichi) can be used both whole and separated. For meat, fish and vegetable recipes discard the husk and lightly crush the seeds before using (unless, of course, otherwise specified). For rice and payes recipes open one side of the cardamom and use whole.

Ginger (adrak) is an essential ingredient in Indian cookery. Ginger root is more preferable than the powdered form.

Chilli powder is hot. Use it sparingly. In many dishes you can omit it altogether. The indiscriminate use of chilli powder spoils the flavour and is foreign to genuine Indian cooking.

Paprika powder adds colour to food.

Cinnamon (dal-chini) powder—cinnamon is used both in stick and powdered forms. It is basically an aromatic and should not be chewed. Similarly take care not to chew cloves (*laung*). Cinnamon, cloves and cardamoms are essentially aromatics.

Some other minor spices like *Fenugreek (methe)*, *nigella indica (kalonji)*, nutmeg (*javatri*), dry *tamarind (imli)*, some shelled nuts such as *almonds, pistachio* are also used in the recipes. Nuts can be easily blanched by soaking them in cold water overnight.

Flours used in the recipes are ordinary white refined (not self-raising) flour, wholemeal flour and besan (gram or chick pea powder).

Fats: Indian food is generally cooked in *ghee (clarified butter)* and in *oil*. I have included a recipe for preparing ghee. When ghee is required for frying, you may substitute by shortening but do not try to cook pilau dishes without having some ghee in hand. You can use any vegetable oil. Never substitute lard for oil.

Yoghourt (Dahi) is widely used in Indian cooking. I have given a recipe for preparing yoghourt at home. Yoghourt used in the recipes is always plain yoghourt.

Measurements used in the recipes

Weights are generally given in tablespoons or teaspoons. Recipes are for 4–6 persons. Increased amounts will require proportionate increase in ingredients other than water. The water becomes relatively less for greater amounts. As to the measurement of the spices and oil, a little variation according to taste would be perfectly in order. In the case of salt, follow your own taste.

Cooking utensils: Ordinary utensils can be used. Two helpful additions would be an Indian tawa (iron griddle) and an Indian kerai (a semi-spherical aluminium or iron pan). The former is useful for making breads and for frying seeds dry (without fat). The latter is very handy for frying food. You can save a lot of oil by using a kerai instead of an ordinary frying pan. Meat and vegetables should be cooked in heavy vessels. Scandinavian casseroles or saucepans made of heavy metal are particularly suited for cooking meat dishes. Heavy aluminium saucepans could also be used for this purpose.

3
Methods for Essential Ingredients

Chhana

1 *quart milk*	or 1½ *tablespoons lemon juice*
¼ *teaspoon (and a little more) citric acid*	2 *tablespoons water*

UTENSILS: one large saucepan; one piece of cheese cloth or fine muslin.

1. Bring milk to boil.
2. When milk rises, pour citric acid (or lemon juice) mixed with water over it. Stir. Milk will break into lumps and liquid.
3. Bring it to boil.
4. Strain through a piece of fine cloth spread over a colander.
5. Squeeze out all the whey.
   This white lump is called chhana, and is used in both sweet and vegetable dishes.

NOTE: You can buy paneer from Indian grocery shops. But paneer, though made in the same way, tends to be stiffer and less easy to work.

Dahi Yoghourt

1 *quart milk*	2 *tablespoons commercial plain yoghourt*

UTENSILS: one large saucepan; one large wide-mouthed flask with lid.

1. Boil milk for 5–6 minutes.

2. Let milk cool until it is slightly warm to the touch.
3. Add natural yoghourt to milk.
   Stir thoroughly with a spoon.
4. Rinse inside of the flask with warm tap water.
   Pour milk into flask and put the lid on.
   Keep it overnight.
5. Open flask.
   Spoon out yoghourt from flask into a glass or earthenware casserole. It will keep fresh for a few days if stored on the bottom rack of the refrigerator.

NOTE:

1. Re: bacterial cultures. These are supplied by the commercial plain yoghourt. Once your own dahi is made, it will form the bacterial cultures for successive preparations, i.e. at least 7 to 8 times. Then buy a plain yoghourt again to get a fresh supply of culture.
2. Yoghourt sets in a mildly warm temperature. The flask retains the warmth of the milk.
3. It can be used in a wide variety of dishes (rice, meat, vegetable, salad) and also is an ingredient for a nourishing, refreshing sherbet. You can also use it as a mildly sour accompaniment for fresh or frozen fruit. Mixed with a little honey, it makes a nice dessert.
4. It is customary in India to make your own yoghourt every day, ready for different purposes.

Ghee (Method 1) Clarified Butter

4 lb. unsalted butter

UTENSIL: one deep saucepan; one glass jar.

1. Put butter into a deep aluminium saucepan on medium to high heat.
2. Reduce heat to low when butter melts and starts to boil.
3. Continue to boil butter.

4. At 10–15 minute intervals, remove the foam from the top of the boiling butter with a large spoon.
5. Boil butter for 30–40 minutes.
   Then remove from heat.
6. When cooled but still liquid, pour the clarified butter into a glass jar, carefully excluding the sediment at the bottom.
7. Once prepared, ghee will keep well for a long time.
   You can easily make enough to last a month or so at a time.
8. 4 lb. unsalted butter will give nearly 7 cups of liquid ghee.
9. When preserved in a jar, ghee sets (turning nearly solid) and looks like other vegetable fats, though with a yellowy colour.

Ghee (method 2) Clarified Butter

4 lb. unsalted butter

UTENSILS: one large saucepan; one glass or earthenware jar.

1. Put butter in the saucepan.
   Put it on the cooker on a low heat.
   Simmer for $1\frac{3}{4}$ hours. Then remove from heat.
2. When the butter is cold but still liquid, throw away the sediment at the top and bottom of the saucepan.
   You can strain it through a piece of thin muslin for greater purity.
   Pour the golden liquid (ghee) into a glass or earthenware jar.
   It will solidify, the speed depending on the room temperature.
   Ghee keeps for a long time.
   4 lb. of butter will produce 7 cups of liquid ghee.

Khoya

1 quart milk

UTENSIL: one large saucepan.

1. Bring milk to boil.
   Go on boiling at medium heat for $1\frac{1}{2}$ hours.
   Stir occasionally.

2. Raise heat to high, stir continuously.
   Within 15 minutes, you will have only a nearly solid substance left at the bottom of the saucepan.
   This is called khoya and is used in sweet dishes.

NOTE: Put a tablespoon of butter at the bottom of the saucepan. Let it melt. Now pour milk in the saucepan. This way you can protect your saucepan from getting a little burnt towards the end of the process.

4

Rice

❧

The word 'rice' is derived from the Tamil. More than a thousand varieties of rices are grown in India and are the staple food of the majority of Indians. In South India, rice is eaten in varied forms at breakfast, lunch and dinner. However, for the last two meals, it is served either plain or fried. Pilaus are generally offered to guests during holidays and for festivals.

The two main types of rice available in Western countries are Patna and Basmati. Although I have used Basmati in my recipes, Patna can be used as well. For cooking Patna, however, you should use a little more water. It is always advisable to wash rice two or three times under the tap, rubbing the grain between the thumb and fingers (use a colander for this purpose).

Plain Rice

1 *cup rice (Basmati or any other*   2 *cups water*
   rice) $\frac{1}{4}$ *teaspoon salt*

UTENSIL: one deep saucepan with cover.

1. Wash rice.
2. Bring water to boiling in saucepan.
   Add salt and rice and cover.
   Cook over low heat. Rice will be ready within 15 minutes.
3. When the rice is cooked and dry, remove from heat and keep half-covered for 5 minutes or so.
4. Serve with any meat or vegetable curry.

NOTE: Basic proportion of rice and water is 1 to 2. This proportion will be followed in all other rice preparations (pilau, khichari or biryani). Some rice may need less water, but this you will find out easily through practice.

Biryani

2 *cups Basmati rice*
1¾ *lb. leg of lamb*
4 *small cloves garlic*
5 *medium-sized onions*
1 *tablespoon fresh grated ginger*
1 *teaspoon coriander powder*
1 *teaspoon cumin powder*
¼ *teaspoon chilli powder*
4 *tablespoons lemon juice*
1 *cup yoghourt*
6 *whole cardamoms*

2 *sticks cinnamon, broken into pieces*
4 *bay leaves*
2 *tablespoons chopped blanched almonds*
1 *tablespoon saffron*
¼ *cup milk*
½ *cup ghee*
9 *cups water*
3 *teaspoons salt*

UTENSILS: one electric blender; one earthenware bowl or casserole; one very large casserole with a lid; one large saucepan; one frying pan.

1. First make marinade as follows.
   Peel and chop coarsely 2 of the onions and all the garlic.
   Put them, with the ginger, in an electric blender.
   Add coriander, cumin, chilli, 1 teaspoon salt and lemon juice.
   Blend at a high speed till you have a smooth paste.
   Put this paste in the bowl and stir in yoghourt.
2. Cut lamb into one-inch pieces and add to the marinade.
   Keep in the refrigerator and marinate at least for 2 hours.
3. Place lamb and marinade in the saucepan. Add ½ cup water.
   Bring to boil.
   Lower heat and simmer for half an hour.
   Remove cover and raise heat to dry up the liquid.
   Boil briskly for half an hour, stirring occasionally.
   At the end you should be left with meat coated with a thick paste.
   Keep meat on one side.

4. Wash rice in a colander.
   Bring to boil $8\frac{1}{2}$ cups of water.
   Add rice and salt.
   Boil briskly for 6 minutes.
   Rice must not cook through.
   Drain rice.
5. Heat ghee in the frying pan.
   Fry 3 onions cut into thin pieces.
   Fry them till they are brown and crisp.
   Remove onions with a perforated spoon and place them on kitchen paper.
   Keep the ghee.
6. Soak saffron in warm milk.
7. Take the big casserole.
   Put $\frac{1}{4}$ cup of water at the bottom.
   Place meat in it.
   Now add a layer of rice followed by a layer of fried onions, bay leaf, cardamoms (opened on one side), almond and cinnamon stick.
   Put in successive layers of rice, fried onions and spices.
   Use half of the fried onions for this purpose.
   Pour the saffron milk over the rice.
   Pour ghee used for frying onions over the rice.
   Place a large piece of aluminium foil over the casserole.
   Place lid over aluminium foil and seal the dish as tightly as you can.
8. Set oven at 300 degrees (Regulo 2). Place casserole in pre-heated oven and bake for 1 hour.
9. Remove casserole from oven.
   Mix meat and rice gently.
   Serve garnished with fried onions on top.

NOTE: Biryani goes well with green salad, cucumber raita and a curry.

Masoor Khichari Rice and Red Lentil Kedgeree

½ cup rice
1 cup red lentils (masoor dhal)
2 tablespoons oil
2 tablespoons ghee
¼ teaspoon cumin seeds
3 bay leaves
1 teaspoon turmeric powder
1"-long piece fresh ginger, thinly
   sliced (optional)
2 teaspoons salt
3 cups water
2 onions, thinly sliced
2 onions, halved
2 small potatoes, halved
½ cup frozen peas
2 tomatoes halved

UTENSIL: one saucepan with a lid.

1. Wash rice and lentils.
   Wash vegetables and peel potatoes.
2. Heat oil in the saucepan.
   Add thinly-sliced onions.
   Fry till they are golden brown.
   Add cumin seeds and bay leaves.
3. Add lentils.
   Fry 2–3 minutes stirring constantly on medium heat.
   Add rice, turmeric, ginger.
   Stir.
4. Add water.
   Add onions, potatoes, tomatoes, peas and salt.
   Cover.
   Bring to boil.
5. Reduce heat to low.
   Simmer for 25 minutes.
   Put ghee on top.
   Serve hot.

Moong Khichari   Rice and Yellow Lentil Kedgeree

½ cup of rice
½ cup moong dhal or yellow lentils
2 tablespoons oil
2 tablespoons ghee
3 whole cardamoms
3 cloves
2 bay leaves
¼ teaspoon cumin powder
¼ teaspoon chilli powder
¼ teaspoon paprika powder
½ teaspoon turmeric powder
1 teaspoon sugar
1½ teaspoons salt
1 small stick of cinnamon, broken into pieces
3 cups water
½ cup frozen peas
2 small potatoes cut into pieces

UTENSILS: one saucepan with a lid; one frying pan or Indian kerai.

1. Place frying pan on high heat.
   Fry lentils (without any fat) for 5 minutes, stirring constantly.
   Wash lentils.
2. Heat oil in the saucepan.
   Add bay leaves, cardamom (opened on one side) and cinnamon.
   Fry for a minute.
   Add washed rice and lentils.
   Add cumin, chilli, paprika, turmeric, sugar and salt.
   Lower heat to medium.
   Fry for 3 or 4 minutes.
3. Add water.
   Add potatoes and peas.
   Cover.
   Bring to boil.
4. Reduce heat to low.
   Simmer for 25 minutes.
   Put ghee on top.
   Serve hot.

Chicken Pilau

2 cups rice (preferably Basmati
  rice)
1 2¼-lb. roasting chicken
2 medium-sized onions
1 cup yoghourt
4 tablespoons almonds
4 whole cardamoms (open them
  on one side)
1 large stick cinnamon broken
  into pieces

8 cloves
4 bay leaves
1½ teaspoons saffron
4 teaspoons salt
3 cups liquid (water + stock, if
  any left)
4 tablespoons ghee

UTENSILS: one large casserole or any oven dish; one saucepan.

MORNING:

1. Joint chicken, after taking off the skin.
   Wash chicken pieces – discard giblets.
   Add ¾ cup of yoghourt, grated onion and 2 teaspoons salt to chicken pieces.
   Boil the whole lot for 20 minutes on low heat.
   Keep this ¾ prepared chicken in refrigerator.
   If there is any stock, pour it into measuring jug and keep it aside.
2. Wash rice and spread on a tray – leave it to dry at room temperature.
3. Peel almonds and cut them into small pieces.

EVENING:

4. Mix rice with the rest of the yoghourt, salt, ghee, cardamom, cinnamon, cloves and bay leaves.
5. In a deep casserole put successive layers of rice, chicken and almond.
   Soak saffron in 2 teaspoons warm water or milk for about 10 minutes.
   Pour it over rice and chicken. Add liquid (including stock, if any).
   Cover the casserole.

6. Set oven at 400 degrees (Regulo 6). Put casserole in the pre-heated oven.

   After 15 minutes, lower heat to 300 degrees (Regulo 2) for one hour.

   Take out the casserole, stir Pilau with a spoon.

   Check that rice is cooked and completely dry.

   Serve hot.

NOTE:

1. Water measurement is usually 1 cup rice to 2 cups water. Deduct the amount of stock, if any, left from the boiled chicken and use it instead of some water. Also make allowance for ghee and yoghourt. I generally take the latter together as equal to 1 cup of liquid.
2. Never cook Pilau with left-over meat.
3. This dish goes well with any curry – meat or vegetable or channa dhal and green salad.
4. If you do not want to spread the work over the day, you can do the whole preparation at one time either in the morning or in the evening.

Lamb Pilau

2 cups Basmati rice
1 lb. leg of lamb
1 onion, grated
2 onions, cut into thin pieces
3 tablespoons sultanas
2 tablespoons almonds
6 cloves
6 whole cardamoms
1 stick cinnamon broken into pieces
2½ teaspoons salt
4 tablespoons yoghourt
6 tablespoons ghee
4 cups water

UTENSILS: one saucepan with a lid; one frying pan; one deep casserole with a lid.

1. Cut lamb into small pieces.
   Mix meat with grated onion and yoghourt.
   Boil with one cup of water on a low heat till meat is tender.

2. Keep meat aside.

   Measure stock (approximately 1 cup) and keep it on one side.
3. Heat ghee in the frying pan.

   Fry almonds and sultanas for 2–3 minutes.

   Keep them aside.
4. In the same ghee, fry onions till they are golden brown.

   Add rice.

   Fry together for 5 minutes.
5. Put mutton in the casserole.

   Pour over rice, fried onion and ghee.

   Add cardamom seeds, cloves, cinnamon sticks and salt.

   Add stock and water (3 cups).

   Cover it.
6. Put casserole in a pre-heated oven set at 300 degrees (Regulo 2).

   Bake one hour.

   See that rice is soft and dry.
7. Serve Pilau garnished with the fried sultanas and almonds.

NOTE: If stock measures more than 1 cup, reduce the amount of water by the same amount.

Pea Pilau

1½ *cups Basmati rice*
2 *cups frozen or fresh peas (if* ¼ *cup ghee or clarified butter*
   frozen, rinse well)
3 *bay leaves*
2 *whole cardamoms (opened on*   *one side)*
                            3 *cups water*
                            1½ *teaspoons salt*

UTENSILS: one frying pan; one deep casserole with cover. (Remember: cooked rice will swell and require more space than when uncooked.)

1. Wash rice.
2. Heat ghee.

   Gently fry rice, peas, bay leaves and cardamom seeds together for 4–5 minutes on medium heat.

3. Pour water on rice mixture and bring to boil.
4. Add salt.
5. When water comes to boil, pour contents into casserole.
6. Put casserole into an oven set at 300 degrees (Regulo 2) for 40 minutes.
   Check that rice is cooked before serving.

Pea-Prawn Pilau

2 *cups Basmati rice*
8 *oz. fresh or frozen prawns*
1 *cup fresh or frozen peas*
3 *tablespoons ghee*
5 *tablespoons yoghourt*
2 *teaspoons salt*

1 *stick cinnamon broken into pieces*
4 *bay leaves*
4 *cloves*
4 *whole cardamoms (opened on one side)*
3 *cups water*

UTENSILS· one mixing bowl; one deep casserole with a lid.

1. Wash rice in the morning.
   Spread on a tray and leave it to dry at room temperature.
2. Wash prawns and peas in cold water till, if frozen, ice is completely melted.
3. Mix all the ingredients, except for water, together.
4. Put them in the casserole.
   Pour water over them.
   Cover.
5. Put casserole in a pre-heated oven set at 300 degrees (Regulo 2).
   Bake one hour.
6. Serve hot.

Saffron Pilau

1½ cups Basmati rice
½ cup ghee
1 cup plain yoghourt
½ cinnamon stick, broken into pieces
2 whole cardamoms (opened on one side)
6 cloves (optional)
1½ tablespoons sultanas, washed

1½ tablespoons chopped pistachio nuts
1½ tablespoons chopped almonds
1 tablespoon cumin seed
1½ tablespoons sugar
1½ teaspoons salt
2 cups water
1 tablespoon saffron

UTENSILS: one deep casserole with cover; one frying pan, preferably iron; one mixing bowl.

1. Wash rice and let it dry at room temperature.
   (Do it in the morning if you are going to cook in the afternoon.)
2. In a mixing bowl put rice, ghee, yoghourt, cardamom, cinnamon, cloves, sultanas, pistachio, almonds, salt and sugar. Mix all these together.
3. Fry cumin seed dry in the frying pan till you can smell the aroma (2–3 minutes).
   Crush it to a powder on a table top and add to the rice mixture.
4. Put the rice mixture into the casserole.
   Add water.
   Sprinkle saffron on the top.
   Stir.
5. Put the casserole into the oven which has been preheated to 400 degrees (Regulo 6).
   After 10 minutes lower the heat to 300 degrees (Regulo 2).
6. After 40 minutes, see whether rice is cooked and dry.
   If not, leave for a few more minutes.
7. Before serving, stir the Pilau.

Chitra-Anna   Coloured Rice

2 cups Basmati rice
1 teaspoon urad dhal
1 teaspoon channa dhal
¼ cup peas
¼ cup green beans
2 medium-sized carrots cut into small pieces
2 cups chopped capsicum (sweet green pepper)
½ teaspoon mustard seed

pinch of hing (asafoetida)
2 tablespoons sultanas
¼ cup cashew nuts
2 lemons (juice)
1 teaspoon turmeric powder
2½ teaspoons salt
2 tablespoons ghee
2 tablespoons oil
3 cups water

UTENSILS: one medium-sized saucepan; one large saucepan.

1. Wash rice. Drain. Mix with turmeric powder.
2. Wash vegetables and boil for 5 minutes. Drain.
3. Heat oil and ghee in a large saucepan.
   Fry cashew nuts and keep them aside.
   Fry sultanas and keep them aside.
   Fry urad dhal and channa dhal till brown.
   Add mustard seeds and fry a minute.
   Add hing.
   Add rice and boiled vegetables.
   Add salt.
   Pour water over rice.
   Cover and cook on low heat.
4. When rice is cooked, add cashew nuts and sultanas.
   Stir well.
   Add lemon juice.
   Serve with raita and papadoms. (If rice is too dry, sprinkle a little more water on it).

NOTE: This delicious dish from Tamilnadu resembles fried rice.

Dosa

3 *cups parboiled rice*
1 *cup urad dhal*

2 *teaspoons salt*

MASALA FOR DOSA

3 *potatoes, peeled and cut into very small pieces*
3 *onions, thinly sliced*
1 *teaspoon urad dhal*
½ *teaspoon mustard seeds*
4 *tablespoons oil*

2 *tablespoons chopped coriander leaves*
2 *green chillies, chopped*
1 *teaspoon salt*
little oil for frying

UTENSILS: one electric blender; one saucepan; one Indian tawa or frying pan (preferably non-stick).

1. Grind rice and dhal together in a blender into a smooth paste. Keep overnight to ferment. (Do not keep it in a cold place.)
2. Heat oil and fry onions for 2–3 minutes.
   Add mustard seeds and fry for a minute.
   Add urad dhal.
   Add potato, salt and green chilli.
   Cover and cook on low heat till the potato is tender.
   Add coriander leaves and keep it aside.
3. Add a little water and salt to rice and dhal paste. This mixture should be the same thickness as a pancake mixture.
4. Heat a little oil in tawa or frying pan.
   Spoon in a little of the mixture and fry like a pancake on both sides.
   When it is golden on both sides put a tablespoon of potato masala in the middle and fold it over (like an omelette).
   When all the dosas are fried, serve them with sambar and coconut chutney.

NOTE:
1. These amounts will make 12 medium-sized dosas.
2. Once rice and dhal mixture has properly fermented it can be

kept in the refrigerator till you are ready to use it. (I generally keep it outside the fridge for at least 18 hours before using.) In the winter, keep it in a bowl wrapped in warm cloth or even stand in an airing cupboard.

3. Dosa, a South Indian dish, is now very popular all over the country. It is particularly suitable for both breakfast and lunch.

Idli

1 *cup parboiled rice*   1½ *teaspoons salt*
1 *cup urad dhal*   *a little ghee*

UTENSILS: one electric blender; one mixing bowl; an egg poacher.

1. Soak rice and dhal for 2–3 hours.
   Grind in a blender into a smooth paste.
   Keep overnight at room temperature.
2. Add salt to the mixture.
   Melt a very little ghee in each egg bowl and then pour in mixture.
   Steam for at least 10 minutes.
   Take out when cool.
   Serve with rasam or sambar.

NOTE:
1. This South Indian recipe makes a good breakfast or lunch dish. You can also steam them in a pressure cooker.
2. When ready idlis resemble little sponge cakes.

Chicken Fried Rice

$1\frac{1}{2}$ cups Basmati rice
$1\frac{1}{2}$–2 cups cooked chicken meat, finely chopped
3 medium onions, thinly sliced
2 eggs
2 long carrots
1 capsicum or green pepper
2 tomatoes

1 shallot (use green portion as well)
$\frac{1}{4}$ cup frozen peas
4 tablespoons ghee
2 teaspoons salt
2 bay leaves
3 cups water for cooking rice

UTENSILS: two saucepans.

1. Cut vegetables into small pieces.
   Wash them.
   Boil carrots for 5 minutes.
   Keep them aside.
2. Hard-boil eggs.
   Cut them into long pieces.
   Keep them aside.
3. Cook rice following the recipe on page 23 for plain rice.
4. Heat ghee in a large saucepan.
   Fry onion pieces till they are golden brown.
   Add bay leaves, peas, shallot, capsicum, boiled carrots and chicken pieces.
   Cook 10 minutes on medium heat.
5. Add rice and salt.
   Fry 5 minutes on medium heat.
6. Serve fried rice garnished with egg and tomato pieces.

Prawn Fried Rice

1½ cups Basmati rice
½ cup frozen, fresh or tinned
   prawns
3 medium onions, thinly sliced
2 long carrots
1 capsicum or green pepper

¼ cup frozen peas
1 shallot
4 tablespoons ghee
2 teaspoons salt
2 bay leaves
3 cups water for cooking rice

UTENSILS: two saucepans.

1. Cut vegetables into small thin pieces.
   Wash them.
   Boil carrot pieces for 5 minutes.
2. Cook rice, following the recipe for plain rice on page 23.
3. Heat ghee.
   Fry onion pieces till they are golden brown.
   Keep aside half fried onion.
4. Add bay leaves and vegetable pieces to onions left in the
   saucepan.
   Add prawns.
   Cook 10 minutes on medium heat.
5. Add rice and salt.
   Fry 5 minutes on medium heat.
6. Serve fried rice garnished with fried onions kept aside.

Vegetable Fried Rice

1½ cups Basmati rice
2 long carrots
1 capsicum or green pepper
¼ cup frozen peas
1 shallot

1 tomato
4 tablespoons ghee
2 teaspoons salt
2 bay leaves
3 cups water for cooking rice

UTENSILS: one deep saucepan; one small saucepan with a lid.

1. Cut carrots into thin small pieces.
   Boil them for 5 minutes.
   Drain.
   Boil peas 3–4 minutes.
   Drain.
2. Cut capsicum (discarding seeds) and shallot into small thin pieces.
   Cut tomato into round pieces.
   Wash them.
3. Cook rice with 3 cups of water on medium heat following the recipe on page 23 for plain rice.
4. Heat ghee in large saucepan.
   Add bay leaves.
   Add carrots, capsicum, shallot pieces.
   Fry 10 minutes on medium heat.
5. Add rice and sugar.
   Fry 5 minutes more on medium heat.
6. Serve garnished with tomato pieces.

NOTE:

1. Sometimes rice in a fried rice gets soggy and pulpy. This danger could be avoided by preparing rice beforehand. Allow rice to cool a little before using it for fried rice.
2. You can use other vegetables such as cauliflower, mushrooms or green beans, treating them like carrots.

5

Bread

Most Indian breads are made of whole wheat or wholemeal flour. While chappati, luchi, puri etc. are made on an ordinary stove, a special clay oven called a tandoor is used for naan. In Punjab, it is usual to have a tandoor or clay oven in the backyard. I have used an ordinary oven as a substitute for a tandoor, with tolerably good results.

Chappati, luchi, puri etc. go very well with most of the meat dishes, vegetables and pulses. For kebabs, I always prepare naan or at least parathas. Indian breads do not go well with fish dishes.

Chappati

2 cups wholemeal flour (atta) $\frac{1}{2}$ *cup (a little more) water*
$\frac{1}{2}$ *teaspoon salt*

UTENSIL: one Indian tawa or heavy frying pan.

1. Mix flour and salt.
   Add water and form the dough.
   Knead for a few minutes.
   Leave for an hour.
2. Knead dough again for at least 5 minutes.
   Divide dough into 12 portions.
   Take one portion and shape it like a ball.
   Roll it out thinly into a circular disc using a little dry flour.
   Do the same with the other portions.

3. Heat the tawa on medium heat and place the chappati (the circular disc) on it.
Wait till the first bubbles appear on the bread.
Turn it over.
Keep it aside.
Do the same with the others.
4. Place chappati in the bottom rack of a preheated oven set at 350 degrees (Regulo 4).
Within 2–3 minutes it will puff up.
You can place 4 or 5 chappatis (side by side) at a time in the oven.
5. Place a heavy napkin in a serving dish.
Stack chappatis in the napkin and fold napkin tightly over to keep them hot.
It is better to eat chappatis as soon as they are prepared.

Luchis

1 *cup plain flour*	¼ *cup (a little more) water*
¼ *teaspoon salt*	*ghee for medium deep frying*
1 *tablespoon ghee*	

UTENSILS: one mixing bowl; one deep frying pan or Indian kerai.

1. Mix flour, salt and ghee.
Add water.
Make a dough and knead it well for several minutes.
2. Divide dough into 14 equal portions.
Shape these into balls.
Roll out each ball thinly in a round shape.
3. Heat ghee in the frying pan.
Place one luchi in ghee.
Put a little pressure in the middle with a frying spoon. It will swell up (some may swell only partly).
Turn over.
Place in the serving dish.

Fry all the luchis.
Serve hot.

Naan   Leavened Bread

2 *cups plain flour*
2 *teaspoons yeast (dry)*
½ *cup warm water*
½ *teaspoon salt*

6 *tablespoons water (approximately)*
¼ *teaspoon kalonji or black onion
   seeds*

UTENSILS: one bowl; one cup; one baking tray.

1. Put yeast in a cup.
   Mix well with warm water.
   Let it stand 10 minutes.
2. Mix flour with salt and kalonji.
   Pour yeast and water mixed with it.
   Add 6 tablespoons water (approximately) and make a stiff dough.
   Knead well.
   Cover and let it stand for 4 hours in airing cupboard.
   Dough will swell and double its size.
3. Knead dough a little.
   Divide dough into 8 pieces.
   Roll out in thin oval shape using dry flour if necessary.
4. Set oven at 450 degrees (Regulo 8)
   Bake each naan in preheated oven.
   Bake first side 3 minutes.
   Turn over and bake second side 2 minutes.
   Keep strict watch over time.
   Naan will swell and have brown spots on both sides.
   Serve hot.

NOTE: Naan goes well with dry meat preparations. It is delicious with tandoori chicken.

Paratha

2 *cups plain flour*	½ *cup water (approximately)*
½ *teaspoon salt*	6 *tablespoons ghee for frying*
3 *tablespoons ghee*	

UTENSILS: one mixing bowl; one heavy frying pan, preferably iron, or an Indian tawa.

1. Make dough. Mix flour, salt and 3 tablespoons ghee thoroughly.
   Now add water.
   Knead well with your hands.
   Knead for 10 minutes.
2. Divide dough into 12 equal portions.
   Take one portion. Roll it out thinly in a round shape.
   Fold it in to make a triangular shape.
   Roll out again keeping triangular shape. Roll out thinly.
   Do the same with each portion.
3. Heat frying pan.
   Place one paratha on the dry pan.
   Wait ½ minute. Turn it over. Wait another ½ minute.
   Add ½ tablespoon ghee. Turn over.
   Fry till paratha has golden brown spots on both sides.
   You can fry 2 parathas at a time.
   Some of the parathas might rise well and some might rise slightly.
4. Serve piping hot with vegetable or meat dishes.

NOTE: The thin variety of paratha described here, as opposed to the thicker North Indian variety, is very popular in Bengal. I personally think it goes better with curry preparations.

Khasta Paratha

2 cups plain flour
½ teaspoon salt
½ cup water (approximately)

2 tablespoons ghee
4 tablespoons ghee for frying

UTENSILS: one large glass or earthenware bowl; one deep frying pan, preferably iron, or an Indian tawa.

1. Make dough with flour, salt, 2 tablespoons ghee and water.
   Knead well with the palm of your hands on a dry surface.
2. Divide dough into 8 equal portions.
   Roll out each portion thickly in a round shape – 4″ diameter.
3. Heat frying pan on medium heat.
   Take one paratha and fry it dry.
   Turn it over.
   Soon you will have golden spots on both sides.
   Add ½ tablespoon ghee.
   Turn paratha over.
   Serve.
   (You can easily fry 2 parathas at a time.)

NOTE: Parathas should be served piping hot with meat or vegetable dishes.

Mughlai Paratha

1½ cups plain flour
¾ teaspoon salt
2 heaped tablespoons ghee
¼ cup (a little more) water

2 eggs
½ small onion
1 green chilli (optional)
4 tablespoons ghee for frying

UTENSIL: one Indian tawa or a heavy frying pan.

1. Beat eggs.
   Cut onion and chilli (discard seeds) into very small thin pieces.
   Mix with egg.
   Add ½ teaspoon salt.

2. Make dough.
   Mix flour, ¼ teaspoon salt, and 2 tablespoons ghee
   Add water.
   Knead well.
   Divide into 8 portions.
3. Take one portion in your hands.
   Shape into a ball.
   Roll out thinly in a round shape.
   Do the same with the rest.
4. Heat frying pan.
   Place one paratha on it.
   Turn it over.
   Place 2 dessertspoons egg mixture on one half of the paratha.
   Fold over the other half (like a stuffed omlette).
   Add ½ tablespoon ghee.
   Fry paratha till it is golden brown on both sides.
   (When you are folding paratha, a little egg might come out.)
   Fry the rest.
   Serve hot.

Aloo Paratha   Potato Paratha

2 cups plain flour	*1 teaspoon finely grated ginger*
2 medium-sized potatoes	*¾ teaspoon salt*
½ onion, finely grated	*15 tablespoons ghee*

UTENSILS: one mixing bowl; one heavy frying pan or Indian
   tawa; one saucepan.

1. Peel potatoes.
   Boil them in salted water till they are soft.
   Mash them.
   Mix them with onion and ginger.
2. Heat 2 tablespoons ghee in the saucepan.
   Add potato mixture.
   Add ½ teaspoon salt.

Cook on medium heat for 5 minutes stirring continuously.
Keep it aside.
3. Mix flour, $\frac{1}{4}$ teaspoon salt.
   Add potato mixture.
   Add 3 tablespoons ghee.
   Mix thoroughly and make a dough with flour and potato mixture.
   Divide it into 10 equal portions.
   Shape these into balls.
4. Roll out each ball in thick round shape – 4" in diameter.
5. Heat frying pan on medium heat.
   Place on paratha on it.
   Cook for 2 or 3 minutes.
   Turn over.
   Cook 2–3 minutes.
   Add 1 tablespoon ghee.
   Turn over and cook till paratha has dark brown spots all over on both sides.
   Do the same with the rest.
   You can fry 2 parathas at a time.
6. Serve hot.

NOTE: Serve potato parathas with a meat or vegetable curry.

Puri

2 cups wholemeal flour
$\frac{1}{2}$ teaspoon salt
2 tablespoons ghee

$\frac{1}{2}$ cup and a little more water
ghee for frying (medium deep)

UTENSILS: one mixing bowl; one deep frying pan or Indian kerai.

1. Mix flour, salt and 2 tablespoons ghee together.
   Mix thoroughly.

Add water.
Make a dough and knead well.
2. Divide dough into 18 equal portions.
   Shape these into balls.
   Roll out each ball in a thin round shape – 3″ in diameter.
3. Heat ghee on medium high temperature.
   When ghee is really hot, place one puri in it.
   With a frying spoon put a little pressure in the middle.
   It will swell up and turn golden.
   Turn it over.
   Place it in the serving dish.
4. Fry all the puris in a similar way.
   Serve hot.

Roti

2 *cups wholemeal flour*   1 *tablespoon ghee*
¼ *teaspoon salt*   ¼ *cup (and a little more) water*

UTENSILS: one mixing bowl; one Indian tawa or heavy frying pan.

1. Mix wholemeal flour with salt and ghee.
   Add water.
   Make a dough and knead well.
2. Divide dough into 6 portions.
   Shape these into balls.
   Roll out one ball thickly in a round shape, 3½″ in diameter.
   Do the same with the rest.
3. Heat frying pan on medium temperature.
   Fry rotis dry for a moment, turning them over.
   Fry each for 1 minute in all.
4. Place them at the bottom rack of a pre-heated oven set at 350 degrees (Regulo 4).
   Keep them there till they swell up (approximately 6–7 minutes).
   Serve straight from the oven.

6

Meat and Poultry

※

In ancient India meat-eating was a normal feature of life. However, there was always a trend towards non-violence in Indian philosophy. With the coming of Buddhism, vegetarianism became the common mode of conduct among the upper castes and even among the common people. However, the tradition of meat-eating continued among the minorities particularly the Muslims; among all communities in some parts of the country like Bengal, Kashmir and Punjab; and among non-Brahmins in other regions.

Hindus generally do not eat beef. My recipes are for lamb but good quality beef could be used without any loss of flavour. The real problem that I faced abroad is that meat there has too much fat. Indian dishes taste better if the fat is trimmed off. Similarly, the fatty outside skin of chickens must always be removed. I have given only those dishes of lamb and chicken which are in common use.

Vindaloo Curry

2 lb. leg of lamb cut into small pieces (trim meat)
3 medium-sized onions, grated
2 medium-sized onions, thinly sliced
1 clove garlic, peeled and grated
2 teaspoons fresh ginger, grated
8 tablespoons white vinegar
1 teaspoon turmeric powder
¼ teaspoon cumin seed
2 bay leaves
2 teaspoons salt
½ cup any vegetable oil or a mixture of vegetable fat and ghee

UTENSILS: one frying pan; one deep casserole with cover; one earthenware or glass pot.

1. Marinate meat with grated onion, garlic, ginger, turmeric and vinegar for an hour or so.
2. Heat fat and fry sliced onion until golden brown.
   Remove fried onion and keep on one side.
3. Fry cumin seed for a minute in the same fat remaining from step 2.
   Add the marinated meat and the spice mixture.
   Add bay leaves.
   Cook briskly for 4–5 minutes on medium heat.
   Add 2 teaspoons salt.
   Pour the whole lot into a casserole and cover.
4. Put the casserole into the oven set at 300 degrees (Regulo 2) for 1 hour.
   Check that meat is tender.
5. Before serving sprinkle fried onion (from step 2) over the meat.

NOTE:

1. Vindaloo curry is a relatively dry dish cooked without water. It goes well with plain rice or with any kind of Pilau.
2. Meat from a good cut of beef can equally well be used.
3. You will find a hotter version of this dish (Vinegar Lamb Curry) on page 57.

Country Curry

2 *lb. leg of lamb*
1 *cup yoghourt*
1½ *teaspoons turmeric powder*
1 *cinnamon stick broken into pieces*
4 *cloves*
6 *whole cardamoms*
6 *tablespoons oil*
4 *tablespoons ghee*

1 *small cauliflower*
2 *medium potatoes*
2"-*long piece fresh ginger*
4 *green chillies (optional)*
4 *onions*
2½ *teaspoons salt*
1 *teaspoon sugar*
1½ *cups water*

UTENSILS: one mixing bowl; one large saucepan with a lid.

1. Cut meat into 1"-cubes.
   Marinate meat with turmeric and yoghourt for 2 hours.
2. Peel potatoes and chop them and cauliflower into medium-sized pieces.
   Cut ginger, onions into thin pieces.
   Cut green chilli into small pieces, discarding seeds.
   Remove husks from cardamoms and crush seeds slightly.
3. Heat oil and ghee together.
   Fry potato and cauliflower pieces separately till they are golden brown.
   Keep them aside.
4. In the same oil and ghee mixture, fry cinnamon stick, cloves and cardamom seeds for 1 minute on medium heat.
   Add onion, ginger and chilli pieces.
   Fry 2 or 3 minutes.
5. Add meat.
   Fry 4–5 minutes stirring frequently.
   Add salt and sugar.
6. Add water.
   Cover and bring to boil. Simmer for 1 hour.
   Add potatoes.
   Cover.
   Simmer for 10 minutes.
7. Add cauliflower pieces.
   Simmer for 10 minutes.
8. Check that meat is tender and serve.

NOTE: Meat from better cuts of beef could be used equally well.

Chappa Curry   Minced Meat Curry

1 *lb. minced meat*	4 *whole cardamoms*
3 *onions, cut into thin slices*	2 *tablespoons ghee*
1 *tablespoon grated ginger*	2 *tablespoons oil*
2 *green chillies, sliced (optional)*	2 *teaspoons salt*
1 *cinnamon stick, broken into pieces*	*juice from 3 lemons*

UTENSILS: two saucepans with lids.

1. Boil minced meat till it is tender (approximately 15 minutes). Drain.
2. Heat ghee and oil together.
   Add cinnamon sticks and cardamom.
   Add onion, ginger and green chilli pieces.
   Fry gently for 3–4 minutes.
3. Add minced meat and salt.
   Fry for 2–3 minutes.
4. Add lemon juice.
   Simmer 7–8 minutes.
   Serve.

Ginger Curry

2 *lb. leg of lamb*	3 *whole cardamoms*
2″*-long piece ginger*	2 *green chillies (optional)*
3 *onions*	½ *teaspoon turmeric powder*
3 *tablespoons vegetable oil*	1 *teaspoon sugar*
1 *stick cinnamon*	2 *teaspoons salt*
3 *cloves*	

UTENSIL: one heavy saucepan with a lid.

1. Slice onion finely.
   Cut ginger into round thin pieces.
   Cut meat into 1″ or smaller cubes.
   Crush cinnamon and cardamom (discarding the husk).

2. Heat oil in the saucepan.
   Put cinnamon, cardamoms and cloves in the pan.
   Fry for a minute.
   Add onion, ginger and green chillies.
3. Add meat and turmeric.
   Fry 2–3 minutes, stirring frequently.
4. Add sugar and salt.
   Cover saucepan.
   Reduce heat to low.
5. Simmer slowly till meat is tender (approximately one hour).
   Serve.

NOTE:

1. No water is needed. It is a relatively dry dish with a flavour of ginger and spices.
2. You can also use a good cut of beef.

Hot Onion Curry

2 *lb. leg of lamb*   1 *cinnamon stick, crushed*
4 *onions, thinly sliced*   4 *whole cardamoms, crushed*
2 *potatoes*   4 *green chillies, cut into small*
2 *teaspoons salt*   *pieces*
½ *cup water*   8 *tablespoons ghee*

UTENSILS: two saucepans with lids.

1. Cut meat into 1″ cubes.
   Peel and cut potatoes into 1″ cubes.
2. Boil meat with salt and water on low heat till meat is tender (approximately one hour).
   Towards the end raise heat so that the juice completely evaporates.
   Stir frequently.
3. Heat ghee.
   Fry potatoes and onions separately till they are golden brown.
   Keep them aside.

4. In the same ghee fry crushed cinnamon and cardamom for
   1–2 minutes.
   Add meat.
   Fry on medium heat.
   Add chilli pieces.
5. Add fried potatoes.
   Reduce heat to low.
   Cover.
   Stir frequently.
6. Cook for 10 minutes till potatoes are tender.
7. Add fried onions.
   Serve.

NOTE: Beef could equally well be used.

Korma Curry

2 lb. leg of lamb	2 teaspoons salt
4 onions, thinly sliced	4 tablespoons ghee
2 tablespoons grated ginger	4 tablespoons oil
3 cloves garlic, grated	5 tablespoons yoghourt
1 teaspoon turmeric powder	½ cup peas (fresh or frozen)
1 teaspoon chilli powder	2 small turnips
2 teaspoons sugar	1½ cups water

UTENSILS: two large saucepans with lids.

1. Simmer meat with water and turmeric till it is tender.
   (Approximately one hour).
   Keep aside meat and liquid separately.
2. Cut turnips into small pieces.
3. Heat ghee and oil together.
   Fry turnip pieces 4–5 minutes.
   Keep them aside.
4. In the same ghee fry sliced onion till it is golden brown.
   Add ginger, garlic, sugar and chilli powder.
   Fry gently on medium heat 1–2 minutes.

5. Add meat.
   Fry 2–3 minutes.
   Add yoghourt.
   Add liquid from the boiled meat.
   Let it come to boil.
6. Add peas, turnip pieces and salt.
7. Cover and simmer till turnips are soft.
   Serve.

NOTE: Meat from a good cut of beef could also be used.

Olathu   Kerala Meat Curry

2 lb. lamb or beef, cut into small squares
½ coconut, shredded fine
3 tablespoons coriander seeds
4 green chillies
1 teaspoon black pepper
4 cardamoms
5 cloves garlic

1 stick cinnamon, broken into pieces
1 teaspoon turmeric powder
2 teaspoons salt
6 onions, thinly sliced
1 teaspoon mustard seeds
8 tablespoons ghee or oil
1 cup water

UTENSILS: one electric blender; two saucepans.

1. Remove cardamom husks and fry seeds with coriander seeds, pepper and cinnamon without any fat for 1–2 minutes.
   Grind together these spices, green chillies and garlic in a blender.
2. Mix meat, coconut, spice paste from step 1, turmeric powder, salt and water.
   Cook on low heat till meat is tender.
3. Heat ghee or oil.
   Fry onions till they are golden brown.
   Add mustard seeds.
   Fry for a minute.
   Add mixture from step 2.

Cook for 3–4 minutes.
Serve.

NOTE: This popular meat dish from Kerala in South India goes well with plain rice.

Lamb Curry

2 lb. leg of lamb
2 medium-sized onions, grated
2 small cloves garlic, grated
1 tablespoon grated ginger
1 cup yoghourt
1 teaspoon turmeric powder
1 teaspoon paprika powder (optional)
1½ teaspoons cumin powder
¼ teaspoon chilli powder
1 tablespoon mustard oil (optional)
2 tablespoons oil
2 tablespoons ghee
2 teaspoons salt
½ teaspoon sugar
2 cups water
2 whole cardamoms

UTENSILS: one mixing bowl; one large saucepan with a lid.

1. Cut meat into small pieces.
   Mix together meat, onion, garlic, ginger, yoghourt, turmeric, paprika, cumin, chilli, mustard oil and marinate for 1–2 hours.
2. Heat oil and ghee mixture in the saucepan.
   Add meat and spices.
   Stir a little.
   Cover and cook on medium heat till juice from meat gets dried.
3. Add water, salt and sugar.
   Cover.
   Simmer for an hour or so till meat is tender.
4. Peel cardamoms and crush the seeds with a rolling pin on a kitchen table top.
   Sprinkle over curry and serve.

NOTE: You can also use a good cut of beef.

Liver Curry

1 *lb. liver*
4 *small onions, crushed or grated*
2 *potatoes*
2 *whole cardamoms*
2 *tablespoons grated ginger*
1 *teaspoon turmeric powder*
½ *teaspoon chilli powder*

4 *tablespoons vinegar*
4 *tablespoons yoghourt*
1 *teaspoon salt*
1 *teaspoon sugar*
3 *tablespoons ghee*
3 *tablespoons oil*

UTENSIL: one saucepan with a lid.

1. Cut liver into small pieces, 1″ long and ½″ wide.
   Peel potatoes and cut into long thin pieces, 1½″ long.
   Wash them.
   Separate cardamom seeds from husks and keep both.
2. Heat oil and ghee together.
   Fry potatoes golden brown and keep them aside.
3. In the same fat fry cardamom seeds and husks for a minute
   on medium heat.
   Add onion.
   Fry for 3–4 minutes.
4. Add ginger, turmeric and chilli powder.
   Add liver pieces.
   Add yoghourt, vinegar, sugar and salt.
   Cover.
5. Simmer for 6 minutes stirring occasionally.
   Add potato pieces.
   Simmer 6 minutes more.
   Serve hot.

Rista Kofta Curry   Meatball Curry

FOR KOFTA:

1 *lb. minced meat*
1 *small onion, grated*
1 *teaspoon grated ginger*
3 *tablespoons yoghourt*

1 *green chilli chopped into pieces*
   (optional)
1 *teaspoon salt*
3 *tablespoons oil*

FOR CURRY:

1 large onion, grated
2 cloves garlic, grated
1 teaspoon grated ginger
1 teaspoon cinnamon powder
4 cloves
3 whole cardamoms

3 tablespoons oil
1 teaspoon sugar
$\frac{1}{2}$ teaspoon salt
$\frac{3}{4}$ cup yoghourt
$\frac{1}{2}$ cup water

UTENSILS: one mixing bowl; two saucepans with lids.

1. First make the koftas.
   Mix together mince, onion, ginger, yoghourt, chilli pieces, salt and 2 tablespoons oil.
   Make 16 balls of minced meat mixed with spices.
   Heat 1 tablespoon oil in the saucepan.
   Place meat balls in the saucepan.
   Cover.
   Simmer for 15 minutes.
   Juice will come out of meat.
   Raise heat to high, uncover.
   Cook till juice gets dried up.
   Keep meat balls aside.
2. Now make curry.
   Heat oil.
   Fry grated onion and garlic till they are golden brown.
   Add cloves, cardamoms, cinnamon.
   Add ginger and fry 1–2 minutes.
   Add salt and sugar.
   Add yoghourt mixed with the water.
3. Place meat balls in curry.
   Cover.
   Bring to boil.
4. Simmer for 15 minutes.
   Serve.

NOTE: Serve with any bread or rice preparation.

Vinegar Lamb Curry

2 lb. leg of lamb, cut into 1"
    cubes
4 medium onions, thinly sliced
4 tablespoons ghee or any vege-
    table oil
3 tablespoons white vinegar
3 large cloves garlic, thinly sliced
3 whole cardamoms
4 cloves
1 teaspoon cinnamon powder
3 bay leaves
1¼ teaspoons salt
4 whole red chillies (optional)

UTENSIL: one deep saucepan with a lid.

1. Fry onion for 2–3 minutes in ghee or oil.
   Add meat, garlic, cardamom, cloves, cinnamon, bay leaves
   and salt.
   Add red chilli after discarding seeds.
   Add vinegar.
2. Fry for 3 or 4 minutes.
   Cover saucepan.
   Reduce heat to low.
   Simmer for 1 hour.
   Check that meat is tender.
   Serve.

NOTE: Meat is cooked in vinegar and its own juice. It goes very
well with rice or bread.

Chilli Meat

2 lb. leg of lamb
4 onions
2 cloves garlic
1 teaspoon turmeric powder
8 green chillies
2 teaspoons salt
3 tablespoons oil
3 tablespoons ghee
1 cup water

UTENSILS: two saucepans with lids.

1. Cut meat into 1" cubes.
   Cut onion in thin pieces.

Crush garlic and half of the green chillies together.
Cut rest of the green chillies into pieces.
2. Mix meat, salt, turmeric and water.
Boil till meat is tender (approximately 1 hour).
Raise heat so that water gets dried up.
3. Heat oil and ghee together.
Fry onions till they are golden brown.
4. Add crushed garlic and chilli.
Stir and fry 2–3 minutes.
Add meat.
Stir and fry 1–2 minutes.
Add chilli pieces.
5. Cook for 20 minutes on low heat.
Serve.

Ginger Stew

2 *lb. leg of lamb cut into cubes*
2 *tablespoons freshly grated ginger*
1 *green chilli, cut into two pieces (optional – but discard the seeds if used)*
2 *bay leaves*
2 *whole cardamoms*
½ *cinnamon stick, broken into pieces*
3 *onions, thinly sliced*

3 *tablespoons ghee*
2 *carrots, chopped into small pieces*
2 *potatoes, chopped into small pieces*
3 *tomatoes, chopped into small pieces*
1 *onion, sliced into large pieces*
2 *teaspoons salt*
2 *cups water*

UTENSIL: one large saucepan.

1. Heat ghee and fry onion (thinly sliced) till golden brown.
Add ginger, chilli, bay leaves, cardamom seeds and cinnamon stick.
Fry for a moment.
2. Add meat and vegetables.
Fry 5 minutes on medium heat.

Add water and salt.
Bring mixture to boil.
3. Lower heat.
Let meat and vegetables cook at a low temperature till meat
is tender.

NOTE: This stew goes well with plain rice or ordinary bread.

Pot Kebab

2 *lb. leg of lamb*
6 *tablespoons yoghourt*
2 *teaspoons coriander powder*
2 *teaspoons cumin powder*
1 *teaspoon turmeric powder*
1 *teaspoon freshly ground black*
 pepper

3 *tablespoons vegetable oil*
3 *tablespoons ghee*
2 *bay leaves*
1 *teaspoon cumin seeds*
1 *teaspoon sugar*
2 *teaspoons salt*
1 *cup water*

UTENSILS: one mixing bowl; one saucepan with a lid.

1. Marinate meat with well-mixed coriander, cumin, turmeric,
black pepper and yoghourt for 2 hours.
2. Heat oil and ghee together.
Fry cumin seeds and bay leaves for a moment on medium
heat.
3. Pour meat and spices into the pan.
Fry gently for 3 or 4 minutes.
Add water.
Let it come to boil.
Add salt and sugar.
4. Reduce heat to low.
Simmer for an hour or so till meat is tender.
Serve.

NOTE: Beef could be substituted for lamb.

Seekh Kebabs

1 *lb. minced meat*
1 *medium-sized onion chopped into thick pieces*
1 *tablespoon coarsely chopped ginger*
2 *teaspoons cinnamon powder*
½ *teaspoon chilli powder*
1 *teaspoon ground mango (am-* *choor) or 2 teaspoons lemon juice*
1½ *tablespoons yoghourt*
2 *tablespoons gram powder (besan)*
2 *tablespoons finely chopped coriander leaves*
1½ *teaspoons salt*

UTENSILS: 8 small metal meat skewers; one electric blender; one mixing bowl.

1. Place onion, ginger, cinnamon and chilli in the blender.
   Blend for 1 minute to make a paste.
   Place it in the bowl.
2. Place minced meat in blender.
   Blend for a few minutes.
   Place it in the bowl.
3. Add ground mango, yoghourt, coriander leaves, salt and gram powder to minced meat.
   Mix all ingredients well.
   Knead well.
4. Put the mixture on a kitchen table top and roll it with your hands like a smooth dough.
   Take a small portion and wrap it round a skewer in a small sausage shape.
   Do the same with the rest.
5. Place the skewers on a grill pan under a very hot grill.
   Turn them over from time to time.
   They should be well-roasted on all sides (approximately 20 minutes).
6. Take kebabs off the skewers and serve hot.

NOTE: Serve with mint or coriander chutney.

Shami Kebabs

1 *lb. minced meat*
½ *cup gram lentils (channa dhal)*
3 *onions, coarsely chopped*
1 *tablespoon grated ginger*
1 *clove garlic, grated*
6 *whole cardamoms*
4 *bay leaves*

1 *cup hot water*
1 *teaspoon salt*
2 *tablespoons chopped mint or coriander leaves (optional)*
1 *egg*
2 *tablespoons oil*

UTENSILS: one saucepan; one frying pan; one electric blender.

1. Mix in a saucepan, meat, gram, onion, ginger, garlic, cardamom, bay leaves and hot water.
   Simmer for an hour till lentils are soft.
   If any liquid is left, raise heat to dry it out completely.
   Let it cool.
2. Run the mixture through electric blender to make a rough paste.
   Alternatively you can use a heavy rolling pin.
3. Mix salt, beaten egg and chopped leaves with the paste.
   Divide it into 16 portions.
   Take one portion in your hands.
   Mould it into an oval shape ¼" thick.
   Do the same with the rest.
4. Heat 1 tablespoon oil in the frying pan on high heat.
   Remove pan from heat.
   Place in many kebabs as possible in the pan.
5. Reduce heat to low.
   Replace frying pan on the cooker.
   Fry kebabs on low heat for 10 to 12 minutes.
   Turn them over from time to time.
   Do not use more fat.
   Each kebab will be crusty outside and soft inside.
6. Fry the rest of the kebabs repeating steps 4 and 5.
7. Serve with a green salad.

NOTE: Kebabs go well with drinks.

Kebabs on Skewers

1 *lb. sirloin steak*
3 *tablespoons yoghourt*
¼ *teaspoon chilli powder*
2 *teaspoons plain flour*
1 *teaspoon salt*

3 *tablespoons vegetable oil*
4 *tomatoes*
3 *capsicums or green peppers*
2 *onions*

UTENSILS: one baking tray; six 10″ long skewers.

1. Cut meat into 1″ pieces.
   Marinate for one hour with yoghourt, chilli and salt.
2. Cut tomatoes, capsicum and onions into 1″ pieces.
   Wash them.
3. Coat meat with flour.
   Put on the skewers first a piece of capsicum, then tomato, onion and meat.
   Fill up skewers by repeating this sequence.
4. Set grill or broiler at 400 degrees (Regulo 6), medium heat.
   Pour oil on the baking tray.
   Place skewers side by side on the baking tray.
   Put it under the preheated grill.
5. Cook for 15 minutes.
   Turn skewers over.
   Cook 10 minutes more.
6. Serve hot.
   Pour kebab liquid left at the bottom of the baking tray over them.

Minced Meat Cutlets

1 *lb. minced meat*	1½ *teaspoons salt*
1 *tablespoon grated ginger*	1 *tablespoon chopped coriander*
3 *medium onions, grated*	*leaves (optional)*
5 *small cloves garlic, grated*	4 *tablespoons gram powder*
1¼ *teaspoons cumin powder*	*(besan)*
1½ *teaspoons cinnamon powder*	1 *egg*
1 *teaspoon turmeric powder*	*breadcrumbs*
½ *teaspoon chilli powder*	*oil for deep frying.*

UTENSILS: one mixing bowl; one deep frying pan.

1. Wash minced meat in a colander. Drain.
   Put it in the mixing bowl.
   Add ginger, onions, garlic, cumin, cinnamon, turmeric, chilli, salt, coriander leaves and gram powder.
   Mix them thoroughly.
2. Divide minced meat mixed with spices into 16 equal portions.
   Take one portion in your hands.
   Press gently and shape into an oval shape approximately ½″ thick.
   Do the same with each portion.
   You have now 16 cutlets to fry.
3. Dip cutlets into beaten egg and crumb them.
4. Heat oil in the frying pan.
   Fry cutlets on medium heat.
   Fry each side 5 minutes.
   Cutlets should be dark brown.
   You can fry 4 to 5 cutlets at a time depending on the size of the frying pan.

Minced Meat 'Chops'

FOR STUFFING:

½ lb. minced meat (good quality lean meat)
2 onions, crushed
4 cloves garlic, crushed
1 teaspoon turmeric powder
½ teaspoon chilli powder

1½ teaspoons ground cinnamon stick
2 tablespoons sultanas
1 teaspoon sugar
salt to taste
1 tablespoon vegetable oil or ghee

FOR POTATO SHELL:

4 medium-sized potatoes
½ teaspoon turmeric powder
1 teaspoon salt

1 tablespoon flour (gram powder – besan – is a good substitute)

FOR FRYING:

1 egg
breadcrumbs

vegetable oil

UTENSILS: one saucepan; one frying pan with a wire basket or an Indian kerai.

STUFFING
1. Heat ghee or vegetable oil.
   Add crushed onions and garlic.
   Fry gently.
   Add minced meat, turmeric, chilli and cinnamon.
   Cook slowly, stirring frequently, without adding any additional water.
2. Stir in sultanas, salt and sugar.
   When completely dry, remove from heat and keep aside.

POTATOES
3. Boil potatoes in jacket in salted water.

4. Peel potatoes and mash thoroughly on a dry kitchen table top.
Add turmeric, flour and salt.
Mix thoroughly in the palm of your hand.
Divide the mixture into 16 equal portions.

SHAPING THE 'CHOPS'

5. Take one portion of potato mixture in your hand.
Shape into a ball, then make a deep well or depression inside the ball pressing sides between fingers and thumb to make a shell similar to an egg cup. Put minced stuffing into the well and bring sides of potato shell together over the stuffing, i.e. enclose meat in potato casing. Do the same with each portion of potato. Now shape them into oval shapes. You now have 16 minced meat 'chops' ready to fry.
6. Heat vegetable oil in the frying pan.
7. Immerse each 'chop' into beaten egg.
Cover each with breadcrumbs.
Fry till 'chops' are golden brown ('chops' should immerse well in the hot oil when frying).

NOTE: Minced meat 'chops' are delicious both hot and cold. Serve with salad, potato crisps and chutney. They make a good savoury to go with drinks.

Minced Meat Koftas

FOR KOFTAS:

1 *lb. minced meat*	1 *teaspoon turmeric powder*
1 *small onion, grated*	1 *teaspoon salt*
1 *teaspoon grated ginger*	3 *tablespoons oil*

FOR CURRY:

1 *large onion, grated*   3 *tablespoons oil*
2 *cloves garlic, grated*   1 *teaspoon sugar*
1 *teaspoon grated ginger*   ½ *teaspoon salt*
1 *teaspoon cinnamon powder*   1 *tomato cut into pieces*
1 *teaspoon turmeric powder*   ½ *cup water*
¼ *teaspoon chilli powder*

UTENSILS: one mixing bowl; two saucepans with lids.

1. First make koftas as follows.
   Mix together minced meat, onion, ginger, turmeric, salt and 2 tablespoons oil.
   Make 16 balls.
   Heat 1 tablespoon oil in the saucepan.
   Place meat balls in the saucepan.
   Cover.
   Simmer for 15 minutes.
   Juice will come out from meat.
   Raise heat to high, uncover.
   Cook till juice gets dried up.
   Keep meat balls aside.
2. Now make curry.
   Heat oil.
   Fry onion and garlic till they are golden brown.
   Add cinnamon, chilli, turmeric, tomato, ginger, salt and sugar.
   Cook for 5 minutes on medium heat.
3. Add water.
   Place meat balls in curry.
   Cover.
   Bring to boil.
4. Simmer for 15 minutes.
   Serve.

NOTE: Serve with any bread or rice preparation.

Minced Meat with Peas

1 lb. minced meat
1 cup peas (frozen or fresh)
2 medium onions, thinly sliced
1 clove garlic, thinly sliced
1 teaspoon turmeric powder
¼ teaspoon chilli powder

½ teaspoon cinnamon powder
½ teaspoon paprika powder
½ teaspoon sugar
2 teaspoons salt
1 tablespoon yoghourt
3 tablespoons oil

UTENSIL: one saucepan with a lid.

1. Heat oil in the saucepan.
   Add garlic pieces.
   Fry till they are brown.
   Add onion pieces.
   Fry till they are golden brown.
2. Add minced meat.
   Add turmeric, chilli, cinnamon and paprika powder and mix well.
   Add yoghourt, salt and sugar.
   Fry on medium heat for 4 or 5 minutes, stirring occasionally.
3. Add peas.
   Cover.
   Cook on medium heat till meat is tender.
   Serve.

Meat Pakoras

1 lb. minced meat
1½ teaspoons cinnamon powder
2½ teaspoons cumin powder
1½ teaspoons turmeric powder
½ teaspoon chilli powder
4 onions, grated
2"-long piece fresh ginger, grated
6 green chillis, cut into small

pieces (optional)
1 tablespoon chopped coriander leaves (optional)
5 tablespoons gram powder (besan)
2 teaspoons salt
1 egg
oil for deep frying

UTENSILS: one mixing bowl; one deep frying pan or Indian kerai.

1. Mix minced meat, cinnamon, cumin, turmeric, chilli powder, onions, ginger, chilli pieces, coriander leaves, and salt.
   Add gram powder.
   Mix thoroughly.
   Add beaten egg.
   Mix thoroughly.
2. Divide minced meat mixture into 22 equal portions.
   Take one portion in your hands.
   Shape it into a round shape – 1½″ in diameter.
   Do the same with other portions.
3. Heat oil for frying.
   First heat it on high temperature.
   When oil is really hot, remove frying pan from the cooker and place 4 or 5 pakoras in oil.
4. Lower heat to medium and place frying pan again on cooker.
   Fry pakoras till they are dark brown on both sides.
   Fry at least for 10 minutes.
   Fry the rest.
   Serve hot.

NOTE: Pakoras are also delicious as a cocktail snack.

Sag Ghosht   Meat with Spinach

2 *lb. leg of lamb*	6 *tablespoons yoghourt*
1 *teaspoon turmeric powder*	1 *teaspoon sugar*
4 *onions, crushed*	2 *teaspoons salt*
2 *cloves garlic, crushed*	3 *tablespoons ghee*
2 *tablespoons grated ginger*	3 *tablespoons oil*
2 *whole cardamoms*	1 *cup cooked spinach*
1 *stick of cinnamon, broken into pieces*	1 *cup water*

UTENSILS: two saucepans with lids.

1. Cut meat into 1" cubes.
   Tear spinach leaves into small pieces.
2. Mix meat and turmeric.
   Add 1 cup water.
   Boil till meat is tender (approximately one hour).
   Keep meat aside.
3. Boil spinach with water.
   Drain well.
4. Heat oil and ghee together.
   Add cardamom and cinnamon.
   Add onion and garlic.
   Cook for 5 minutes stirring occasionally.
   Add ginger.
5. Add meat, yoghourt, salt and sugar.
   Cook for 5 minutes on medium heat.
6. Add boiled spinach.
   Cook for 15 minutes more stirring occasionally.
   Serve.

NOTE: Beef could equally well be substituted.

Chicken Curry

3 lb. 10 oz. chicken
6 tablespoons natural yoghourt
2 medium-sized onions, grated
½ teaspoon fresh ginger, grated
1 teaspoon turmeric powder
¼ teaspoon chilli powder
½ tablespoon mustard oil (optional)
½ teaspoon cumin seed

2 tablespoons or so of ghee or vegetable oil
salt to taste (approximately 2½ teaspoons)
2 medium-sized potatoes, peeled and halved. (The number of potatoes will depend on how many you want to serve per head)

UTENSILS: one glass or earthenware bowl; one saucepan; one big casserole with a cover.

1. Take off skin and cut chicken into pieces.
   Wash pieces.
   In the glass bowl mix chicken pieces with yoghourt, onion, ginger, turmeric, chilli and mustard oil.
   Marinate for half an hour or more.
2. Heat ghee or vegetable oil in the saucepan.
   Fry potatoes till they are golden brown.
   Keep them aside.
   Fry cumin seed in the same oil for a minute or so.
3. Pour chicken and marinade in the saucepan.
   Fry for 3 or 4 minutes.
4. Pour contents of saucepan into the casserole.
   Place potatoes (from step 2) over the meat.
   Cover it and put it in a preheated oven set at 300 degrees (Regulo 2).
   Cook for 50–60 minutes. Check whether chicken and potatoes are tender.
   Serve with rice.

NOTE: You could omit step 4. In that case, continue cooking as in step 3. Add 1 cup of water and cook over medium heat till chicken is tender.

Chicken Curry with Coconut

3½ *lb. chicken*
1 *cup unsweetened coconut (des-
    sicated or freshly grated)*
3 *medium onions, grated*
1 *tablespoon ginger, grated*
3 *medium cloves garlic, grated*
4 *tablespoons vegetable oil*
1 *teaspoon turmeric powder*

½ *teaspoon paprika*
½ *teaspoon cinnamon powder*
3 *tablespoons yoghourt*
3 *whole cardamoms*
4 *cloves (optional)*
1 *teaspoon sugar*
1 *teaspoon salt*
2 *cups boiling water*

UTENSILS: one glass bowl; one large saucepan with a lid.

1. Soak coconut in 2 cups boiling water for 1 hour.
   Run through electric blender to squeeze out milk.

Strain through a piece of fine cloth.
Discard coconut fibre.
Keep aside coconut milk.
2. Skin chicken and joint into pieces. Wash.
Marinate with well-mixed yoghourt, turmeric, paprika and cinnamon for 1 hour.
3. Heat oil in the saucepan.
Fry grated onion and garlic till they are light brown.
Add ginger.
Add cardamoms and cloves.
Add chicken and marinade.
Cook on medium heat for 15 minutes with the lid on.
4. Take off lid.
Raise heat.
Boil till liquid in the saucepan has evaporated.
Add coconut milk.
Add salt and sugar.
Bring to boil.
5. Lower heat to medium.
Cook till chicken is tender, 20 minutes or more (approximately).
Serve.

Chicken Cutlets

2 lb. 6 oz. chicken
2 onions, finely grated
2 tablespoons finely grated fresh ginger
3 green chillies, cut into pieces (optional)
1 teaspoon turmeric powder
1 teaspoon cinnamon powder

1½ teaspoons cumin powder
¼ teaspoon chilli powder
2 tablespoons gram powder (besan)
1½ teaspoons salt
1 egg
breadcrumbs
oil for deep frying

UTENSILS: one saucepan; one mixing bowl; one frying pan or Indian kerai; one electric blender.

1. Boil chicken with water and a little salt.
2. Bone the chicken.
   Blend chicken meat at high speed till it is smoothly minced.
3. Mix chicken meat with onions, ginger, chilli pieces, turmeric, cinnamon, cumin, chilli powder and gram powder. Add salt.
   Mix thoroughly.
   Divide into 10 portions.
4. Take one portion in your hands.
   Mould into an oval shape – ¼" thick.
5. Dip into beaten egg and cover with breadcrumbs.
   Do the same with the rest.
6. Heat oil on high heat.
   Remove frying pan from the cooker and place as many chicken cutlets as possible in oil.
7. Reduce heat to medium.
   Replace frying pan on cooker.
   Fry cutlets till they are dark brown on both sides.

NOTES:
1. You can use stock of the boiled chicken for making clear soup.
2. Serve cutlets with green salad or with rice and curry preparations.

Chicken-Garlic

3 *lb.* 10 *oz. chicken*
1½ *cups plain yoghourt*
4 *cloves garlic*
1 *teaspoon chilli powder*

4 *tablespoons oil (any vegetable oil)*
2 *tablespoons plain flour*
3 *teaspoons salt*

UTENSILS: one large earthenware pot or casserole; one large baking tray.

1. Take skin off the chicken.
   Join it and wash the pieces, discarding giblets.
   Crush garlic after peeling off skin.

2. Marinate chicken pieces with half of yoghourt, half of garlic, half of chilli powder and salt.
   Place in earthenware pot or casserole and keep overnight in the refrigerator (not in the freezing compartment).
3. Next day take the marinated chicken out of the refrigerator 2–3 hours before cooking.
4. Set the oven at 400 degrees (Regulo 6).
5. Add the rest of the yoghourt, crushed garlic, chilli powder and flour to the marinated chicken and mix thoroughly.
6. Arrange chicken pieces on a baking tray.
   Pour the spice and yoghourt mixture over it.
   Pour oil over the chicken pieces.
7. Put the baking tray in the preheated oven.
   Lower heat to 350 degrees (Regulo 4) after half an hour.
   Turn over the chicken pieces.
8. Cook for another half hour or so till the chicken is tender.

NOTE: This dish is dry. It goes well with green salad and crispy bread. It is a very good savoury for a drinks party.

Chicken Pakoras

1¾ lb. *chicken breast*
2 *onions, grated*
2 *cloves garlic, grated*
2 *teaspoons grated ginger*
2 *teaspoons salt*

14 *tablespoons gram powder (besan)*
1 *teaspoon salt*
1 *pinch baking soda*
13 *tablespoons water*
oil for deep frying

UTENSILS: one mixing bowl; one frying pan.

1. Skin chicken.
   Cut into small pieces.
   Wash.
2. Mix chicken pieces with onions, garlic, ginger and salt.
   Marinate for 4 hours or more. (Keep it in the refrigerator.)
3. Make batter with gram powder, salt, baking soda and water.

4. Heat oil (high heat).
Remove pan from the cooker.
Dip chicken pieces into batter and place them in hot oil.
You can fry 3 or 4 pieces at a time.
Turn them over.
5. Lower heat to medium.
Replace pan on cooker.
Cover.
Fry for 10 minutes on medium heat.
6. Uncover.
Fry 5 minutes more on medium heat turning over chicken pieces occasionally.
Fry the rest.
Serve hot.

NOTE: Chicken pakoras are delicious as a cocktail snack.

Chicken Tandoori

3 lb. 6 oz. chicken

INGREDIENTS TO SOAK CHICKEN IN:

2 tablespoons lemon juice   *½ teaspoon salt*

INGREDIENTS FOR MARINADE:

1 cup yoghourt   *1 teaspoon ginger powder*
2 teaspoons paprika powder   *4 small cloves garlic, crushed*
2 teaspoons coriander powder   *3 tablespoons vegetable oil*
2 teaspoons cumin powder   *1 teaspoon salt*

INGREDIENTS FOR GARNISHING:

¾ teaspoon caraway seeds   *3–4 drops cochineal*
2 teaspoons lemon juice

UTENSILS: one earthenware bowl or big casserole; one baking tray; one frying pan.

1. Wash and skin chicken, discard giblets.
   Prick it all over with a sharp kitchen knife.
   Mix lemon juice and salt.
   Rub them into the chicken and leave for half an hour.
2. Mix paprika, cumin, coriander, ginger, salt, garlic, yoghourt
   and oil.
   Rub chicken thoroughly inside and outside with this marinade.
   Marinate for 6–8 hours.
3. Set oven at 500 degrees (Regulo 9). Remove the extra spices
   and put chicken on the middle shelf of the pre-heated oven.
   Put a baking tray on the bottom shelf.
   Roast for 25 minutes.
4. Fry caraway seeds on a dry frying pan for 2 or 3 minutes till
   you can smell the aroma.
   Grind them on a dry kitchen table top with a rolling pin.
   Mix this powder with lemon juice and a few drops of red
   colouring (Cochineal).
5. Take out chicken. Rub it with this paste and roast it 10
   minutes more.
   Serve.

NOTE: Serve Tandoori chicken with rice or a bread like naan
and tomato-onion salad. It is a completely dry dish. You can
also cook Tandoori on a spit roaster.

Chicken in Yoghourt

3½ lb. chicken	slices
3 long carrots, cut into small pieces	1 teaspoon lemon rind, cut into thin slices
2 medium-sized potatoes, peeled and cut into small pieces	1 teaspoon flour
	4 tablespoons ghee
1 tablespoon grated ginger	1 cup yoghourt
2 onions, cut into thin slices	½ cup water
3 cloves garlic, cut into thin	1½ teaspoons salt

UTENSIL: one large heavy saucepan with a lid.

1. Skin chicken.
   Discard giblets, wash.
   Tie legs and wings.
2. Heat ghee in the saucepan.
   Add garlic.
   Add onion.
   Fry 1–2 minutes.
3. Dust chicken lightly with flour.
   Place it in the saucepan.
   Fry chicken, onion, garlic together for 5 minutes on high heat.
4. Mix yoghourt with water.
   Pour over chicken.
   Add ginger, carrots and potatoes.
   Add lemon rind pieces.
   Add salt.
5. Bring to boil.
   Cover.
   Lower heat.
   Simmer.
6. After ½ hour turn chicken over.
   Simmer for another ½ hour.
   Serve.

Chicken Dopiaza   Onion Chicken

3 lb. chicken	1 cup plain yoghourt
4 medium-sized onions, thinly sliced	½ teaspoon sugar
2 medium-sized onions, grated	2 teaspoons salt
½ teaspoon turmeric powder	¼ cup ghee
½ teaspoon chilli powder	½ cup water

UTENSILS: one frying pan; one saucepan; one casserole with a lid.

1. Remove the skin and joint chicken.
   Wash chicken pieces.
2. Mix chicken with half of the turmeric powder and half of the
   grated onion.
   Boil chicken in pan for 15 minutes on medium heat with half
   a cup of water.
3. Arrange chicken pieces in the casserole.
   Keep aside any water left from step 2.
4. Heat ghee in the saucepan.
   Add sliced onion and fry till golden brown.
   Put fried onion aside.
   Add grated onion to fat.
   Fry till it is golden brown.
   Add sugar, chilli, remaining half of the turmeric and salt.
   Add yoghourt and any water left from step 2.
   Stir the mixture of spices and yoghourt.
5. When the spice mixture comes to boil, spread it over the
   chicken pieces in the casserole.
6. Put the casserole in the preheated oven set at 300 degrees
   (Regulo 2).
   Cook for 50–60 minutes.
   Before serving, sprinkle the fried onion from step 4 all over
   the chicken pieces.

NOTE: Pineapple goes well with this dish. If you have a can of
   pineapple chunks, fry them till golden brown. Arrange the
   fried pineapple pieces on the top of the chicken before
   serving.

Fried Chicken

2¼ lb. chicken breast	2 teaspoons salt
2 medium-sized onions, crushed	2 eggs
1½″-long piece ginger, crushed	breadcrumbs
6 tablespoons yoghourt	oil for deep frying

UTENSILS: one mixing bowl; one deep frying pan or Indian kerai.

1. Remove skin from chicken breasts.
   With a sharp knife take out bones.
   Cut chicken meat into small pieces.
2. Mix chicken pieces with onions, ginger and yoghourt.
   Keep overnight (in the refrigerator).
3. Add salt to chicken.
   Dip one piece in breadcrumbs.
   Then dip it into beaten egg and crumb again.
   Do the same with the rest.
4. Heat oil on high heat.
   Remove frying pan from the cooker and place as many chicken pieces as possible in the very hot fat.
   Turn them over.
5. Reduce heat to medium.
   Replace frying pan on the cooker.
   Cover and fry for 6 minutes.
6. Take off cover and fry 4 minutes more, turning chicken pieces over.
   Fry the rest.
   Serve.

NOTE: Fried chicken goes well with a green salad. It is delicious as a cocktail snack.

Grilled Chicken Indian Style

3 *lb. 5 oz. chicken*	1 *teaspoon turmeric powder*
2 *onions, grated*	1½ *teaspoons cumin powder*
2 *tablespoons grated ginger*	1 *teaspoon paprika powder*
3 *cloves garlic, grated*	2¼ *teaspoons salt*
1 *cup yoghourt*	4 *tablespoons oil*

UTENSILS: one mixing bowl; one grill pan and grid.

1. Skin chicken.
   Cut into pieces.
   Wash.
2. Mix with onion, ginger, garlic, yoghourt, turmeric, cumin, paprika, oil and salt.
   Marinate for 6 hours (keep in refrigerator).
3. Heat grill (high).
   Place chicken on the grid.
   Place under grill.
4. Baste chicken pieces with marinade from time to time. Turn them over.
5. Cook for 45 minutes.
   Serve hot.

NOTE: This recipe is particularly suitable for barbecues. Serve with green salad.

7

Fish and Eggs

❧

Fish is eaten in many parts of India, particularly the coastal regions. The Bengalis, for example, are well known as 'fish-eaters'. In a market in Calcutta, I once counted twenty-five different kinds of fish, most of them freshwater varieties.

Some types of fish are available in the West which taste like those available in India: for instance, carp resembles rohi and shad resembles hilsa. I have given only those recipes which will suit fish available in England and America. Lobster, prawn and shrimp are, of course, universal.

Fish 'Chops' (method 1)

6 oz. salmon or tuna fish
2 medium potatoes
1 onion, thinly sliced
1 tablespoon fresh ginger, thinly sliced, or 1 teaspoon ginger powder

3 green chillies cut into small pieces (optional)
salt to taste
1 egg
breadcrumbs
oil for deep frying

UTENSILS: one saucepan; one deep frying pan.
1. If fresh fish is used, boil till it is tender.
   Remove skin and bones and then mash it.
2. Boil potatoes in salted water and then peel.
   Mash them and mix well with fish.
   Add onion, salt, ginger and chilli pieces.
   Mix thoroughly.
3. Divide potato–fish mixture into 10 portions.
   Shape them with your hands into round shapes ¼″ thick.

4. Beat egg.
   Dip fish 'chops' in egg.
   Cover them with breadcrumbs.
5. Deep fry them on medium heat.
   They should be golden brown.

NOTE: Serve fish 'chops' with rice and salad.

Fish 'Chops' (method 2)

FOR STUFFING:

1 lb. filleted fish	½ teaspoon salt
1 large onion, thinly sliced	½ teaspoon sugar
1 teaspoon thinly-sliced ginger	10 peanuts roasted in shells
1 green chilli, thinly sliced (optional)	(optional)
	4 tablespoons vegetable oil
1 tablespoon sultanas	

FOR POTATO SHELL:

1 big and 2 medium potatoes	1 small onion, grated
½ teaspoon salt	1 tablespoon flour

FOR FRYING:

1 egg	oil for deep frying
breadcrumbs	

UTENSILS: one saucepan; one deep frying pan or Indian kerai.

STUFFING:

1. Boil fish for 5 minutes.
   Drain.
   Mash thoroughly.
2. Heat oil.
   Fry onion till golden brown.

Add fish, ginger, green chilli, sultanas, salt, sugar, peanuts (discard shells).
Fry for 5 minutes.
Keep aside.

POTATO SHELL:

3. Boil potatoes in jacket in salted water.
4. Peel.
 Mash thoroughly on a dry surface.
 Add grated onion, salt and flour.
 Mix thoroughly in the palm of your hands.
 Divide potato mixture into 12 separate portions.

SHAPING:

5. Take one portion of potato in your hand.
 Shape into a ball.
 Then make a deep well or depression inside the ball, pressing up sides between fingers and thumb so a shape like an egg-cup is formed.
 Put fish stuffing into the well and bring sides of potato shell together over the stuffing and enclose fish in potato casing.
 Do the same with each portion of potato.
 Now shape them into oval shapes $\frac{1}{2}''$ thick.
 You have now 12 fish 'chops' ready to fry.
6. Heat oil in the frying pan.
7. Immerse each 'chop' in beaten egg.
 Cover each with breadcrumbs.
 Fry till 'chops' are golden brown.

NOTE: A good idea is to shape 'chops', cover them with breadcrumbs and put them in the refrigerator for 2 or 3 hours to allow them to settle before frying. This way you can be sure of their not breaking while frying.

Fish Curry

1 *lb. haddock fillet*
3 *tomatoes*
½ *cup peas (fresh or frozen)*
¼ *teaspoon chilli powder*
1 *teaspoon turmeric powder*
2 *tablespoons oil*
2 *tablespoons ghee*

½ *teaspoon methe (fenugreek)*
1 *green chilli (optional)*
1 *tablespoon chopped coriander leaves*
1 *teaspoon salt*
¾ *cup water*

UTENSIL: one saucepan with a lid.

1. Cut fish into 8 pieces.
   Chop tomatoes into small pieces.
2. Sprinkle a little turmeric and salt over fish pieces.
3. Heat oil and ghee together.
   Add methe.
   Add fish pieces.
   Add chilli, turmeric, tomatoes and peas (rinse well if frozen).
4. Add water and green chilli.
   Bring to boil.
   Simmer for 15 minutes.
5. Add coriander leaves.
   Serve.

NOTE: Serve with plain rice. Halibut is especially suited to this particular dish too.

Korma Curry

1 *lb. haddock or any other fillet*
1 *onion, crushed or finely grated*
1 *teaspoon turmeric powder*
½ *stick cinnamon, crushed*
3 *whole cardamoms, crushed*
1½ *teaspoons finely-grated ginger*
¼ *teaspoon chilli powder*

1 *teaspoon salt*
½ *teaspoon sugar*
6 *tablespoons yoghourt*
5 *tablespoons oil*
¾ *cup water*
2 *teaspoons ghee*

UTENSIL: one saucepan with a lid.

1. Cut fillet into 6 pieces.
   Wash.
   Sprinkle with turmeric powder and a little salt.
2. Heat oil.
   Add crushed cinnamon and cardamoms (discarding the shell).
   Add onion.
   Fry for 2 or 3 minutes.
   Add ginger, chilli, salt, sugar and yoghourt.
   Cook for 3 or 4 minutes on medium heat.
3. Add fish pieces.
   Cook for 2 or 3 minutes.
4. Add water.
   Bring to boil.
   Cover and simmer for 15 minutes.
   Pour liquid ghee over fish.
   Serve.

NOTES:
1. Serve with a rice or bread preparation.
2. Halibut is particularly suitable for this recipe.

Herring Curry

4 *large herrings*
1 *aubergine*
¼ *teaspoon kalonji (black onion seeds)*
1 *green chilli (optional)*
1½ *teaspoons turmeric powder*
2 *teaspoons cumin powder*
3 *teaspoons salt*
¾ *cup water*
6 *tablespoons oil*
oil for medium deep frying
1 *tablespoon coriander leaves (optional)*

UTENSILS: one saucepan with a lid; one frying pan.

1. Take off heads.
   Cut each herring into 4 pieces.
   Cut aubergine into medium-sized pieces.
   Discard stems of coriander.
   Wash.

2. Sprinkle ½ teaspoon turmeric and 1 teaspoon salt over fish.
   Heat oil and fry pieces for 2–3 minutes each.
   Keep them aside.
3. Heat 6 tablespoons oil in the saucepan.
   Add kalonji and chilli.
   Add aubergine pieces.
   Fry for 3–4 minutes.
   Stir in turmeric and cumin.
4. Add water and remaining salt.
   Bring to boil.
   Add fish.
   Cover.
   Cook on medium heat for 15 minutes.
   Turn fish over once.
5. Add coriander leaves.
   Serve.

NOTE: Serve with plain rice.

Shrimp Curry

12 *large shrimps*	1½ *teaspoons cumin powder*
1 *large potato*	¼ *teaspoon chilli powder*
2 *medium tomatoes*	1 *teaspoon salt*
1 *onion, grated*	5 *tablespoons oil*
½ *tablespoon grated ginger*	¼ *cup water*
½ *teaspoon turmeric powder*	

UTENSIL: one saucepan with a lid.

1. Remove shells.
   Make a cut on the back of each shrimp and take out the black thread.
   Peel potato and chop into small pieces.
   Cut tomatoes into small pieces.
2. Heat oil.
   Fry shrimps for 3–4 minutes.
   Keep them aside.

3. In the same oil, fry onion till it is golden brown.
   Add potatoes and tomatoes.
   Add ginger, turmeric, cumin, chilli and salt.
   Cook for 5 minutes on medium heat.
4. Add water.
   Add shrimps.
   Bring to boil.
   Lower heat.
   Simmer for 15 minutes on medium heat.
   Serve.

NOTE: Serve with plain rice or a variety of bread.

Daimach   Fish with Yoghourt

1½ lb. carp
1 cup yoghourt
1 stick cinnamon, broken into pieces
2 whole cardamoms
4 cloves
1½ tablespoons sultanas
1½ tablespoons sugar
1 teaspoon salt
2 tablespoons ghee
2 tablespoons vegetable oil
1 tablespoon fresh grated ginger
2 green chillies, cut into pieces (optional)

UTENSILS: one earthenware or glass bowl; one saucepan.

1. Cut fish into 6 long pieces.
   Wash thoroughly.
   Marinate fish in yoghourt for 1 hour.
2. Heat oil and ghee together in the saucepan.
   Add cinnamon, cardamom, cloves and sultanas.
   Fry 2–3 minutes.
3. Take fish out of yoghourt and place in the saucepan.
   Cook 3–4 minutes.
   Pour yoghourt over fish.
   Add salt and sugar.
4. Simmer for 30 minutes.
   Add ginger and chilli.

Simmer 5 minutes.
Serve.

NOTE: Fish is cooked in yoghourt without any water. You can use any white fish like, for instance, haddock. Cut white fish into larger pieces.

Fish Fry

1 *lb. haddock or any other fillet*	1 *teaspoon salt*
¼ *teaspoon turmeric powder*	1 *egg*
1 *onion, grated*	*breadcrumbs*
2 *teaspoons grated ginger*	*oil for medium deep frying*

UTENSILS: one mixing bowl; one frying pan.

1. Cut fillet into 6 pieces.
   Wash.
2. Add ginger, onion, turmeric and salt to fish.
   Marinate for 4 hours.
   (Keep in the refrigerator.)
3. Cover fish pieces with breadcrumbs.
   Dip them into beaten egg.
   Dip them again in breadcrumbs.
4. Heat oil on high heat.
   Remove frying pan from cooker.
   Place fish pieces in hot oil.
5. Lower heat to medium.
   Replace frying pan on the cooker.
   Fry till fish pieces are dark brown on both sides.
   (You can fry 3 to 4 pieces at a time.)
   Serve hot.

Herring Jhal   Herring with Mustard

4 *large herrings*   *pieces (optional)*
1½ *teaspoons turmeric powder*   2 *small onions, finely sliced*
6 *tablespoons oil*   1 *cup water*
4 *tablespoons mustard*   3 *teaspoons salt*
2 *green chillies, cut into small*   *oil for medium deep frying*

UTENSILS: one frying pan; one saucepan; one electric blender.

1. Take off heads.
   Cut each herring into 4.
   Wash.
2. Heat oil.
   Sprinkle ½ teaspoon turmeric and 1 teaspoon salt over fish.
   Fry them for 2–3 minutes on high heat.
   Keep them aside.
3. Blend mustard and chilli pieces together using some of the water allowed in the recipe.
4. Place 6 tablespoons oil in the saucepan (you can use oil in which fish was fried).
   Heat it.
   Add onion slices.
   Fry them till they are golden brown.
   Add mustard–chilli, water, and rest of turmeric and salt.
5. Bring to boil.
   Add fish.
   Cover.
   Simmer on low medium heat for 15 minutes.
   Serve.

NOTE: Serve with plain rice.

Haddock with Tomato

2 medium haddock fillets, cut into pieces 2½" long (any other fillet will do)
6 tablespoons oil
3 small onions, grated
1 tablespoon thinly-sliced fresh ginger
1 green chilli (optional)

4 medium tomatoes, cut into small pieces
¾ teaspoon salt
1 teaspoon sugar
plain flour
1 tablespoon chopped coriander leaves (optional)

UTENSIL: one deep frying pan with a lid or heavy casserole.

1. Flour fish pieces lightly.
   Heat oil.
   Fry fish pieces, 1 minute each side.
   Keep them aside.
   Cut green chilli in half.
2. Fry onions light brown.
   Add ginger, green chilli, tomato pieces, salt and sugar.
   Add fish pieces.
   Cover.
3. Cook for 15 minutes at medium heat.
4. Decorate with fresh coriander leaves if you have any and serve.

NOTE: Fish is cooked in tomato juice without any water. Serve with bread or rice.

Lobster Malaicurry   Lobster with Coconut

2 *fresh lobsters*
1 *cup dessicated unsweetened coconut*
5 *tablespoons oil (any vegetable oil)*
1 *medium onion, grated*
1 *clove garlic, grated*
1 *teaspoon fresh ginger, grated*
½ *teaspoon turmeric powder*
a pinch of chilli powder (op-tional)
¼ *teaspoon paprika powder*
3 *tablespoons yoghourt*
a pinch clove powder
¼ *teaspoon cinnamon powder*
2 *whole cardamoms (grind seeds)*
½ *teaspoon salt*
1 *teaspoon sugar*
1½ *cups hot water*

UTENSILS: two saucepans; electric blender.

1. Soak dessicated coconut in hot water for two hours.
   Put in blender for ½ minute to squeeze out milk.
   Strain through a piece of muslin.
   Discard coconut fibres and keep aside coconut milk.
2. Boil lobsters for one hour.
   Take off heads.
   Break shells.
   Cut lobster flesh into small pieces.
3. Heat oil in a saucepan.
   Add grated onion and fry till golden brown.
   Add grated garlic and continue to fry.
   Add lobster pieces, ginger, turmeric, chilli, paprika, clove, cinnamon, cardamom and yoghourt.
   Fry for 15 minutes at medium heat.
4. Add coconut milk. Add sugar and salt. Bring to boil.
5. Cook for 15 minutes at medium heat.
   Serve.

NOTE: Lobster malaicurry could be served with bread or rice.
   Use lobster heads for frying (see recipe on page 91).

Fried Lobster Heads

2 *lobster heads, boiled*	1 *egg*
½ *onion, grated*	*breadcrumbs*
½ *teaspoon turmeric powder*	*oil for frying*
½ *teaspoon chilli powder*	*salt to taste*

UTENSIL: one frying pan.

1. Take heads of boiled lobsters.
   Take off shells.
   Marinate lobster heads with grated onion, turmeric, chilli and salt for one hour.
2. Dip lobster heads first in beaten egg and then in breadcrumbs.
3. Heat oil in frying pan.
   Add lobster heads.
   Reduce heat to low.
4. Fry on both sides till they are golden brown.
   Serve.

NOTE: Fry heads when you are cooking lobster malaicurry. In that way you will use up every portion of the lobster.

Prawn with Spring Onion

16 *prawns or large shrimps*	2 *teaspoons cumin powder*
2 *bunches spring onions*	¼ *teaspoon chilli powder*
¼ *teaspoon kalonji (black onion seeds)*	1 *teaspoon salt*
	6 *tablespoons oil*
1 *teaspoon turmeric powder*	¾ *cup water*

UTENSIL: one saucepan with a lid.

1. Remove heads of prawns.
   Wash.
   Cut green parts of spring onions into small bits (do not use the onion itself).
   Wash.

2. Heat oil.
   Fry prawns for 2–3 minutes.
   Keep them aside.
3. In the same oil fry kalonji seeds for a moment.
   Add spring onions (green parts).
   Add turmeric, cumin, chilli and salt.
   Fry for 3–4 minutes.
4. Add prawns.
   Add water.
   Bring to boil.
   Cover and simmer for 15 minutes.

NOTE: Serve with plain rice.

Dai-Sarse-Chingri   Prawn cooked in Yoghourt and Mustard

1 *lb. prawns or large shrimps*	1 *teaspoon turmeric*
2 *tablespoons mustard seeds*	1 *teaspoon salt*
4 *green chillies (optional)*	2 *tablespoons oil*
4 *tablespoons yoghourt*	¼ *cup water*

UTENSILS: one casserole with a lid; electric blender.

1. Shell the shrimps.
   Make a cut along their backs and take out the black thread.
   Wash.
2. Blend mustard seeds, chilli and water in an electric blender.
   Keep covered an hour in a cup.
3. Mix fish, mustard mixture, yoghourt, turmeric, oil and salt
   in the casserole.
4. Place the casserole in a preheated oven set at 350 degrees
   (Regulo 4).
5. Lower heat to 300 degrees (Regulo 2) after half an hour.
6. Bake half an hour more.
   Serve with rice.

Prawn Cutlets

12 *prawns or large shrimps*	1 *egg*
2 *onions, grated*	*breadcrumbs*
1 *tablespoon grated ginger*	*oil for deep frying*
½ *teaspoon salt*	

UTENSILS: one mixing bowl; one frying pan.

1. Take off shells but leaving tail-section of the shell.
   Make a cut down the back.
   Press down with the knife (do not cut into halves).
   Shrimp will spread flat with one side joined.
   Make a few pricks on the flesh with a knife.
2. Marinate shrimps for 2 hours or more in grated onion, ginger and salt (keep in refrigerator).
3. Cover each cutlet with breadcrumbs, then into beaten egg.
   Cover with breadcrumbs again.
4. Heat oil on high heat.
   Remove frying pan from the cooker.
   Place 4 or 5 cutlets in the oil (number will depend on the size of the pan).
5. Reduce heat to medium.
   Replace pan on the cooker.
   Fry for 10 minutes turning cutlets over from time to time.
   Fry the rest.
   Serve.

NOTE: Serve with a green salad. It also makes a good savoury to accompany drinks.

Egg Curry

6 *hard-boiled eggs*
2 *medium-sized potatoes, peeled*
   and cut into 6 pieces
2 *medium-sized onions, grated*
1 *teaspoon fresh grated ginger*
1 *bay leaf*
1 *teaspoon turmeric powder*
1 *teaspoon cumin powder*

4 *tablespoons plain yoghourt*
½ *cup water*
salt to taste (1 teaspoon approxi-
   mately)
2 *tablespoons vegetable oil*
1 *tomato, cut into 4 pieces*
   (optional)

UTENSIL: one saucepan.

1. Boil eggs and potatoes for 8–10 minutes.
   Drain water.
   Shell the eggs.
2. Heat oil.
   Fry onion till golden brown.
   Add ginger, bay leaf, turmeric, cumin, yoghourt and salt.
   Fry for 2 or 3 minutes.
   Add ½ cup water.
   Bring to boil.
3. Add eggs and potato.
   Cook for 10 minutes on low heat.

NOTE: Serve with plain rice or with bread.

Egg Dum

6 *eggs*
1 *onion, grated*
1 *teaspoon cumin powder*
1 *teaspoon paprika powder*

1 *teaspoon turmeric powder*
3 *tablespoons yoghourt*
3 *tablespoons oil*
1 *teaspoon salt*

UTENSIL: one saucepan with a lid.

1. Hard-boil eggs.
   Shell them.
   Cut each into 4 pieces.

2. Heat oil.
   Fry onion till it is golden brown.
   Add cumin, paprika, turmeric, yoghourt and salt.
   Add egg slices.
3. Cover and simmer for 10 minutes.
   Serve.

Egg-Jhal   Egg-Mustard

6 *eggs*
3 *tablespoons ready-made mus-*
   tard
1½ *teaspoons paprika*

1 *teaspoon turmeric*
1 *teaspoon salt*
¼ *cup water*
4 *tablespoons oil*

UTENSIL: one casserole with a lid.

1. Hard-boil eggs.
   Shell them.
2. Put oil in the casserole.
   Place eggs in it carefully.
3. Mix water, mustard, paprika, turmeric and salt.
   Pour over eggs.
   Cover casserole.
4. Place casserole in a preheated oven set at 350 degrees
   (Regulo 4)
   Bake one hour.

NOTE: Serve with rice. It is a relatively dry dish.

8

Vegetables

✣

A very wide variety of vegetables is available in India. Vegetables and green leaves like coriander are everyday items for both rich and poor. Since frozen food is uncommon, whichever vegetables are used depends on the season. Thus, vegetables familiar in England like cauliflower, cabbage and so on, are winter foods while the summer has its own products. Bengal is particularly rich in vegetables, and in this section I have drawn largely on the Bengali style of cooking in which very few spices and little water is used. I have included only recipes for those vegetables which are available in England and America.

Aloo-Chilli   Potato-Chilli

2 *large potatoes*	1 *teaspoon sugar*
1 *stick cinnamon, broken into pieces*	1 *teaspoon salt*
4 *whole cardamoms*	2 *tablespoons oil*
4 *green chillies*	2 *tablespoons ghee*
	½ *cup water*

UTENSIL: one medium-sized saucepan with a lid.

1. Peel potatoes and chop into 1″ cubes.
   Cut chillies into small pieces (wash off seeds).
2. Heat oil and ghee together.
   Add cinnamon sticks and cardamom seeds.
   Add chilli pieces.

Add potato pieces.
Fry for 2 or 3 minutes.
3. Add water, salt and sugar.
Cover.
Bring to boil.
4. Cook on low heat for 15 minutes.
Serve.

Aloo Dum

7 *medium-sized potatoes* $\frac{1}{4}$ *tablespoon yoghourt*
1$\frac{1}{2}$ *tablespoons grated ginger*   2$\frac{1}{2}$ *teaspoons salt*
2 *onions, grated*   1 *lemon (juice)*
1 *teaspoon cumin seeds*   3 *tablespoons oil*
1 *teaspoon turmeric powder*   3 *tablespoons ghee*
$\frac{1}{4}$ *teaspoon chilli powder* $\frac{1}{2}$ *cup water*

UTENSIL: one saucepan with a lid.

1. Boil potatoes in jackets and then peel them.
Cut them into halves.
2. Heat oil and ghee.
Add onion.
Fry till golden brown.
Add ginger.
Add cumin seeds.
Fry a minute.
Add yoghourt, turmeric and chilli powder.
Fry on medium heat for 4–5 minutes.
3. Add water.
Add potatoes.
Bring to boil.
Add salt.
Simmer for 15 minutes.
4. Add lemon juice.
Simmer for 3–4 minutes.
Serve.

Potatoes with Onions

3 *medium-sized potatoes*	1 *teaspoon turmeric powder*
2 *medium-sized onions*	¼ *teaspoon chilli powder*
4 *tablespoons oil*	1½ *teaspoons salt*

UTENSIL: one saucepan with a lid.

1. Peel potatoes and cut into small thin pieces.
   Cut onions into thin pieces.
2. Heat oil in the saucepan.
   Add onion pieces.
   Fry 1 or 2 minutes.
3. Add potato pieces.
   Add turmeric, chilli and salt.
   Cover.
4. Cook on medium heat stirring occasionally.
   Check that potatoes are tender (approximately 7–8 minutes).
   Serve.

NOTE: It is a dry dish.

Aloo Chokha   Mashed Potato

2 *medium-sized potatoes*	1 *teaspoon salt*
2 *onions, thinly sliced*	3 *tablespoons ghee or oil*
½ *lemon (juice)*	

UTENSIL: one saucepan.

1. Boil potatoes in skins.
   Cool.
   Peel and mash thoroughly.
2. Heat oil in the saucepan.
   Fry onion till golden brown.
3. Add mashed potato and salt.
   Cook for 1 or 2 minutes stirring constantly.

4. Add lemon juice.
Cook 2 minutes more on medium heat stirring constantly.
Serve.

Potato 'Chops'

4 *medium potatoes*	1½ *tablespoons thinly sliced*
1 *medium onion, cut into thin*	*ginger*
pieces	1 *egg*
1 *green chilli, cut into small*	1 *teaspoon salt*
pieces	*oil for medium deep frying*

UTENSILS: one saucepan; one frying pan.

1. Boil potatoes in jackets.
Peel.
Mash thoroughly.
2. Mix mashed potatoes with onion, ginger, chilli, salt and beaten egg.
3. Heat oil.
Take a little potato in your hands, lightly shape it into a ball (like a walnut), place it in oil.
Place as many potato 'chops' as you can in oil.
Fry on medium high heat till they are brown all over.
Serve hot.

NOTE: They are a good snack at teatime or with drinks.

Potato Pakoras

2 *large potatoes*	½ *teaspoon chilli powder*
7 *tablespoons gram powder*	1¼ *teaspoons salt*
(besan)	*pinch of baking soda*
½ *teaspoon kalonji (black onion*	6½ *tablespoons water*
seeds)	*oil for deep frying*

UTENSILS: one mixing bowl; one frying pan or Indian kerai.

1. Peel potatoes.
   Cut them into thick round pieces – $\frac{1}{4}''$ thick.
2. Make a batter mixing gram powder, kalonji, chilli powder, salt, baking soda and water.
   Mix thoroughly.
3. Dip potato pieces in batter.
4. Heat oil on high temperature.
   Remove frying pan from the cooker and place potato pieces into oil (as many as possible).
5. Reduce heat to medium.
   Place frying pan on the cooker.
6. Fry potato pieces till they are brown on both sides.
   Serve hot.

NOTE: It is a good snack at teatime or with drinks.

Artichoke Hearts Curry

14 oz. artichoke hearts (tinned)
1 large potato
$\frac{1}{4}$ teaspoon cumin seeds
1 teaspoon cumin powder
$\frac{1}{4}$ teaspoon chilli powder
$1\frac{1}{2}$ teaspoons coriander powder
$\frac{1}{2}$ teaspoon turmeric powder
$\frac{1}{4}$ teaspoon cinnamon powder
3 small whole cardamoms

3 cloves (optional)
1 teaspoon grated ginger
3 tablespoons yoghourt
6 tablespoons vegetable oil
1 teaspoon ghee (optional)
$1\frac{1}{2}$ teaspoons sugar
$\frac{1}{2}$ teaspoon salt
1 cup boiled water

UTENSIL: one saucepan with a lid.

1. Squeeze out preservative from each heart and wash it thoroughly by holding flower side towards the tap.
   Peel potato and cut it into slices $1''$ thick.
2. Heat oil.
   Fry potato golden brown.
   Add artichoke hearts.
   Fry for 2–3 minutes.

Add cumin seeds.
Fry 1 minute.
3. Mix with $\frac{1}{4}$ cup of water all the spices – cumin powder, chilli, turmeric, cinnamon, coriander.
Pour it over artichoke hearts and potatoes.
Add cardamom seeds, cloves, ginger, yoghourt, salt and sugar.
Fry at medium heat for 5 minutes.
4. Pour in boiled water.
Cook at medium heat till potatoes are soft.
Add ghee and serve.

Aubergine Curry

1 *medium aubergine, cut into 6 long pieces*	$\frac{1}{2}$ *teaspoon cumin powder*
6 *tablespoons oil for frying*	$\frac{1}{2}$ *teaspoon salt*
1 *teaspoon grated ginger*	$\frac{1}{2}$ *teaspoon sugar*
$\frac{1}{2}$ *teaspoon turmeric powder*	2 *tablespoons oil for curry*
$\frac{3}{4}$ *teaspoon coriander powder*	$\frac{1}{2}$ *cup water*

UTENSILS: one frying pan; one saucepan with a lid.

1. Heat 6 tablespoons oil in the frying pan.
Fry aubergine pieces till they are dark brown.
Keep them aside.
2. Heat 2 tablespoons oil in the saucepan.
Add ginger, turmeric powder, coriander and cumin.
Fry for 2–3 minutes on medium heat.
3. Add water.
Add salt and sugar.
4. Bring to boil.
Place the aubergine pieces in carefully.
Cover.
5. Cook for 10 minutes on medium heat.
Serve.

Egg-Plant or Aubergine Chakya   Aubergines in Lemon

2 *medium-sized aubergines*	1 *teaspoon turmeric powder*
2 *potatoes*	1 *teaspoon salt*
4 *tablespoons vegetable oil*	1 *lemon (juice)*
1 *teaspoon cumin seeds*	$\frac{1}{2}$ *cup water*
1 *teaspoon cumin powder*	

UTENSIL: one saucepan with a lid.

1. Cut aubergine into 1″ pieces.
   Peel potatoes and cut into 1″ pieces.
   Wash them.
2. Heat oil.
   Add cumin seeds.
   Fry them for $\frac{1}{2}$ minute.
   Add vegetables.
   Add cumin powder, turmeric and salt.
   Fry on medium heat for 3–4 minutes.
3. Add water and cover the saucepan.
   Cook on medium heat.
4. When potatoes are soft add lemon juice.
   Serve.

Brinjal Bhartha   Grilled Aubergine

1 *large aubergine*	1 *teaspoon salt*
1 *onion, cut into thin slices*	2 *tablespoons oil*

UTENSILS: one grill pan; one frying pan.

1. Wash aubergine.
   Dry it.
2. Grease grill pan.
   Put aubergine under grill
   Turn occasionally, holding it by its top.
   The aubergine will become soft inside and the skin will go
   black (approximately 20 minutes).

Place it under running cold water and peel by hand.
Mash well.
Keep it aside.
3. Heat oil.
Fry onion till it is golden brown.
Add mashed aubergine and salt.
Cook for 6 minutes.
Serve.

Beguni   Fried Aubergine in Batter

1 *medium-sized egg-plant or aubergine*	1 *teaspoon turmeric powder*
1 *teaspoon salt*	½ *cup oil (any vegetable oil suitable for frying)*

FOR BATTER:

4½ *tablespoons plain flour*	2 *teaspoons oil*
1 *tablespoon Bisquik or any cake mixture*	½ *teaspoon salt*
	½ *cup water*

UTENSILS: one frying pan; one mixing bowl.

1. Cut aubergine into half lengthwise.
   Take one half and slice it into pieces ¼″ thick.
   Do the same with the other half.
   Wash the pieces. Drain them.
   Add salt and turmeric powder.
2. Make batter with flour, cake mixture, oil, salt and water.
   Mix thoroughly.
3. Heat oil in the frying pan.
   Dip aubergine pieces into the batter one at a time and put them in the hot oil.
   Fry as many at a time as can be arranged easily in the frying pan.
   The exact number will depend on the size of the pan.

4. Keep temperature at medium heat and fry aubergine pieces till they are golden brown.

NOTE: Serve with plain rice and a meat dish. On its own it is good at teatime or with drinks.

Banana Kofta Curry

FOR KOFTAS:

2 green cooking bananas*
1 onion, finely grated
½ tablespoon finely grated ginger
¼ teaspoon chilli powder
½ teaspoon salt

1 tablespoon flour
oil for deep frying

*available at Indian and West Indian grocers

FOR CURRY:

1 onion, sliced
½ tablespoon grated ginger
1 teaspoon cumin powder
½ teaspoon paprika powder
½ teaspoon turmeric powder
3 whole cardamoms
3 cloves

½ teaspoon cinnamon
½ teaspoon sugar
¾ teaspoon salt
3 tablespoons oil
1½ cups water
1 medium tomato, chopped

UTENSILS: two saucepans with lids; one frying pan.

1. Boil banana in skin in salted water for 20 minutes.
   Peel.
   Mash banana thoroughly.
   Remove cardamom husks and crush seeds lightly.
2. Mix mashed banana, onion, ginger, chilli, salt and flour.
   Mix thoroughly.
   Divide banana into 12 equal portions.
   Take each portion in your hands and shape like a ball pressing softly.

3. Heat oil. Fry banana balls till they are dark brown.
   Keep them aside.
4. Now make curry. Heat 3 tablespoons oil.
   Fry onion till it is golden brown.
   Add ginger.
   Add cumin, paprika, turmeric, cardamom seeds, cloves,
   cinnamon and tomato pieces.
   Fry 2–3 minutes.
   Add salt and sugar.
5. Add water and bring to boil.
   Boil for 5 minutes on medium heat.
   Add banana balls.
   Bring to boil.
6. Simmer for 10 minutes and serve.

NOTE: This delicious curry goes well with any rice or bread
preparation.

Banana Curry

2 *cooking bananas**   3 *tablespoons yoghourt*
1 *medium potato*   1 *teaspoon salt*
¼ *teaspoon cumin seeds*   3 *tablespoons oil*
½ *teaspoon turmeric powder* ½ *cup water*
½ *teaspoon paprika powder*
1 *teaspoon cumin powder*   *available at Indian and West Indian
1 *teaspoon grated ginger*   grocers

UTENSIL: one saucepan with a lid.

1. Peel bananas.
   Cut into small pieces.
   Peel potato and cut into small pieces.
   Wash.
2. Heat oil.
   Fry cumin seeds for a minute.
   Add potato and banana.

Add turmeric, paprika, cumin, ginger, yoghourt and salt.
Fry on medium heat for 5 minutes.
3. Add water.
Bring to boil.
Simmer for 15 minutes.
Serve.

Green Beans

10 oz. frozen green beans or 1½
    cups fresh beans chopped
    into ½"-long pieces
½ teaspoon turmeric powder
¼ teaspoon mixture of cumin
seeds, kalonji seeds and methe
    or only cumin seeds
1 teaspoon prepared mustard
½ teaspoon sugar
3 tablespoons oil

UTENSILS: two saucepans.

1. Cook beans according to instructions on packet. If fresh boil
till tender in salted water.
Add turmeric powder to water.
Drain.
2. Heat oil in the saucepan.
Add mixture of seeds.
Fry for 1–2 minutes.
Add beans, salt, sugar and mustard.
3. Cook for 5 minutes on low heat.
Serve.

Cabbage with Prawn or Shrimp

1 medium-sized cabbage, thinly
    shredded
2 medium-sized potatoes, peeled
    and diced
1 lb. shrimps or prawns: remove
    shells and stomach thread
½ cinnamon stick, cut into pieces
1 teaspoon turmeric powder
2 teaspoons cumin powder
½ teaspoon chilli powder
¼ cup ghee (or any vegetable oil)
¼ cup milk
2 teaspoons flour
1½ teaspoons salt

UTENSIL: one large saucepan with a lid.

1. Heat ghee.
   Fry shrimps or prawns for 3–4 minutes.
   Put them aside.
2. Add potatoes.
   Fry them on a high heat till they are golden brown.
   Put them aside.
3. Add cabbage to the fat already used for frying prawns and potatoes.
   Add cinnamon stick and salt.
   Fry 1 minute.
4. Lower heat to medium.
   Add turmeric, cumin, chilli, potatoes and salt.
   Stir.
   Cover tightly.
5. Continue cooking, occasionally stirring cabbage in the pan.
   When cabbage is tender, add prawns or shrimps.
   Cover.
6. Continue cooking till the cabbage's own water is nearly dried up.
   Mix milk and flour in a cup.
   Pour it over the cabbage.
   Cook for a minute or so.
   Serve hot.

NOTE: Cabbage is cooked in its own liquid.

Cabbage with Peas

1 *small cabbage*	1½ *teaspoons grated ginger*
½ *cup peas (frozen or fresh)*	½ *teaspoon sugar*
1 *large potato*	1 *teaspoon salt*
½ *stick cinnamon, broken into small pieces*	3 *tablespoons oil*
	¼ *cup water*
2 *bay leaves*	3 *tablespoons milk*
1 *teaspoon turmeric powder*	½ *teaspoon flour*
1½ *teaspoons cumin powder*	2 *teaspoons ghee or butter*
¼ *teaspoon chilli powder*	

ÚTENSIL: one saucepan with a lid.

1. Shred cabbage into thin pieces.
   Peel and cut potato into small pieces.
2. Heat oil in the saucepan.
   Add cinnamon and bay leaves.
   Add potatoes.
   Fry for 3–4 minutes.
   Add cabbage.
   Add turmeric, cumin, chilli, ginger, sugar and salt.
   Fry on medium heat for 5–6 minutes.
3. Add water.
   Add peas.
   Cover.
   Simmer for 15 minutes.
4. Mix milk, flour and liquid ghee.
   Pour over cabbage.
   Cook 2 or 3 minutes more.
   Serve.

Cabbage 'Chops'

1 *small cabbage*
4 *medium potatoes*
1 *onion, cut into very small pieces*
1 *teaspoon very finely grated ginger*
½ *teaspoon paprika powder*

1 *teaspoon turmeric powder*
2 *teaspoons salt*
5 *tablespoons gram powder (besan)*
oil for medium deep frying

UTENSILS: one saucepan with a lid; one frying pan.

1. Cut cabbage into thin slices.
   Boil till it is tender.
   Drain.
2. Boil potatoes in jackets.
   Peel.
   Mash them thoroughly.

3. Mix cabbage, mashed potato, onion, ginger, paprika, turmeric, salt and gram powder.
   Mix thoroughly, crushing cabbage with your hands.
4. Take a little cabbage mixture and shape it into a flat round shape, $\frac{1}{2}''$ thick and $1\frac{1}{2}''$ in diameter.
   Do the same with the rest of the cabbage mixture.
5. Heat oil in the frying pan on high heat.
   Remove frying pan from the cooker and place as many cabbage patties as you can do comfortably.
6. Reduce heat to medium.
   Replace frying pan on the cooker.
   Turn over 'chops'.
   Fry them till they are dark brown on both sides.
   Fry the rest.
   Serve hot.

NOTE: You can make 'chops' with cauliflower following the same recipe.

Stuffed Cabbage

1 *medium-sized cabbage*	*sliced*
1 *lb. minced meat*	1 *clove garlic, finely sliced*
$\frac{1}{2}$ *teaspoon turmeric powder*	$\frac{1}{2}$ *teaspoon ginger powder*
$\frac{1}{2}$ *teaspoon chilli powder*	$1\frac{1}{2}$ *tablespoons oil*
$\frac{1}{2}$ *teaspoon cinnamon powder*	2 *tablespoons ghee*
2 *whole cardamoms*	2 *teaspoons salt*
2 *medium-sized onions, finely*	1 *teaspoon sugar*

UTENSILS: one large saucepan; one deep frying pan; one large casserole.

1. Boil water in a large saucepan.
   Add 1 teaspoon salt. Remove saucepan from heat.
   Place cabbage in the water and leave for one hour.
2. In the meantime prepare minced meat.
   In the frying pan, put 1 tablespoon oil and 2 tablespoons ghee.

When the mixture is hot, fry sliced garlic.
When garlic is light brown, add sliced onion.
When it is golden brown add minced meat, turmeric, chilli,
cinnamon, cardamom, ginger, salt and sugar.
Fry them on a high heat, stirring well, for 2–3 minutes.
Cover the frying pan and lower heat to medium.
Minced meat will be cooked in its own liquids.
When completely dry, keep it aside.
It will take 15–20 minutes to prepare minced meat.

3. After one hour, take cabbage out of the salted water.
Cut off a piece at the bottom.
Scoop out the hard centre and make a hole big enough to
contain minced meat.
Put minced meat into the hole and cover it with cabbage
leaves.

4. Put ½ tablespoon oil in casserole.
Place cabbage in the centre and put casserole in a pre-heated
oven set at 300 degrees (Regulo 2).
From time to time, see whether there is any water in the
casserole; if so, throw it away.

5. After 15–20 minutes, put casserole under the grill to brown
cabbage lightly.
Serve hot.

Cauliflower Curry

1 *medium-sized cauliflower*
2 *potatoes*
½ *cup frozen or fresh peas*
2 *green chillies (optional)*
¼ *teaspoon fresh grated ginger*
¼ *teaspoon cumin seeds*
1 *teaspoon cumin powder*

1 *teaspoon turmeric powder*
¼ *teaspoon garam masala (optional)*
1 *teaspoon salt*
½ *cup water*
¼ *cup vegetable oil*

UTENSILS: one saucepan.

1. Separate cauliflower into spears.

Peel potatoes and cut into chunks.

Slit chillies open and remove seeds.

2. Heat vegetable oil.

Fry cauliflower pieces till they are brown (fry a few at a time – cover them while frying to save both time and oil).

Keep them aside.

Fry potatoes in the same oil.

When potatoes are brown, add cumin seeds.

Fry for a minute, add turmeric, cumin powder, garam masala, green chilli, grated ginger and salt, stirring well.

Fry for a minute or so.

Add water.

3. When it is boiling, add cauliflower and peas.

4. Cover the saucepan and cook for 8–10 minutes.

Check that cauliflower and potatoes are tender.

Serve with rice or bread.

Kashmiri Cauliflower

1 medium-sized cauliflower cut into 4 pieces

½ teaspoon turmeric powder

¼ teaspoon (or a bit less) asafoetida (hing)

1 green chilli, cut into pieces

1 teaspoon ginger pieces

3 teaspoons sugar

1¾ teaspoons salt

2 tomatoes, cut into pieces

1 tablespoon chopped coriander leaves

1 cup oil for frying

UTENSILS: one frying pan; one saucepan with a lid.

1. Heat oil in the frying pan.

Fry cauliflower pieces sprinkled with a little salt and turmeric till they are dark brown.

2. Place 6 tablespoons oil from the oil used for frying cauliflower into the saucepan.

Add asafoetida.

Add chilli, ginger and tomato pieces.

Add salt and sugar.
Cook for 4 minutes on medium heat.
3. Add cauliflower pieces.
Stir well.
Cover.
Simmer 30 minutes.
Uncover.
Cook one minute stirring well.
Sprinkle coriander leaves at the top.
Serve.

Cauliflower Roast

1 *medium-sized cauliflower*	1 *teaspoon garam masala*
6 *tablespoons yoghourt*	4 *whole cardamoms, ground*
1½ *tablespoons grated ginger*	1½ *teaspoons salt*
1 *clove garlic, grated*	1½ *teaspoons sugar*
½ *teaspoon cinnamon powder*	4 *tablespoons vegetable oil*

UTENSILS: one earthenware or glass bowl; one baking tray or casserole.

1. Clean cauliflower after taking off all leaves.
Discard cardamom husks and lightly crush seeds.
2. Marinate whole cauliflower, after pricking it a little with a fork, with well-mixed yoghourt, ginger, garlic, cinnamon, garam masala, cardamom, sugar and salt for 2 hours in a glass or earthenware bowl.
3. Set oven at 400 degrees (Regulo 6). Put cauliflower in the middle of the baking tray.
Pour all the spices and yoghourt over it.
Pour oil in.
Put the baking tray in the pre-heated oven.
4. Reduce heat to 300 degrees (Regulo 2) after 15 minutes.
Cook for 1 hour and 20 minutes.
Check that cauliflower is tender.

5. Put cauliflower in the tray under grill for 15 minutes to brown.
6. Serve as it is or decorated with thinly-sliced fried potatoes.

Cauliflower Pakoras

½ medium-sized cauliflower
7 tablespoons gram powder
  (besan)
½ teaspoon kalonji (black onion
  seeds)

½ teaspoon chilli powder
1¼ teaspoons salt
pinch of baking soda
6½ tablespoons water
oil for deep frying

UTENSILS: one mixing bowl; one frying pan or Indian kerai.

1. Cut cauliflower into 12 medium-sized pieces.
2. Make a batter mixing gram powder, kalonji, chilli powder, salt, baking soda and water.
   Mix thoroughly.
3. Dip cauliflower pieces in batter.
4. Heat oil well on high temperature.
   Remove frying pan from the cooker and place cauliflower pieces into oil (as many as possible).
5. Reduce heat to medium.
   Place frying pan on the cooker.
6. Fry cauliflower pieces till they are light brown all over.
   Serve hot.

NOTE: It is also a good snack for teatime or as a savoury with drinks.

Chhana Dalna   Indian Cheese Curry

2 quarts milk for chhana
1 cup peas (fresh or frozen)
2 small tomatoes, cut into pieces
2 onions, grated
2 teaspoons grated ginger
1 teaspoon paprika powder

1 teaspoon cumin powder
1 teaspoon turmeric powder
1 teaspoon cinnamon powder
1 teaspoon salt
8 tablespoons oil
1 cup water

UTENSIL: one saucepan (medium or small) with a lid.

1. Make chhana with 2 quarts milk following the recipe given on page 19.
2. Knead chhana with your hands for 3–4 minutes to make it smooth.
   Press it down flat – $\frac{1}{2}$" thick.
   Make horizontal cuts followed by vertical cuts at $\frac{1}{2}$" distance.
   You now have small chhana cubes.
3. Heat oil.
   Fry chhana cubes on medium heat till they are golden brown on both sides.
   Keep them aside.
4. In the same oil fry grated onions till they are golden brown.
   Add ginger and tomatoes.
   Add paprika, cumin, turmeric, cinnamon, salt and peas.
   Fry for 3–4 minutes on medium heat.
5. Add water.
   Bring to boil.
   Simmer for 10 minutes.
6. Add chhana pieces.
   Simmer for 10 minutes more.
   Serve.

NOTE: Serve with plain rice or a bread preparation.

Bhindi Bhaji   Curry with Ladies' Fingers

$\frac{1}{2}$ *lb. ladies' fingers or okra*
1 onion grated
1 teaspoon grated ginger
$\frac{1}{2}$ *teaspoon turmeric powder*
$\frac{1}{2}$ *teaspoon paprika powder*

1 teaspoon cumin powder
2 tablespoons yoghourt
3 tablespoons oil
$\frac{1}{2}$ *cup water*
1 teaspoon salt

UTENSIL: one saucepan with a lid.

1. Cut off tops of ladies' fingers.
   Wash.

2. Heat oil.
   Fry onion till golden brown.
   Add ladies' fingers.
   Add ginger, turmeric, paprika, cumin, yoghourt and salt, stirring well.
   Cook on medium heat for 5 minutes.
3. Add water.
   Bring to boil.
   Lower heat.
   Simmer for 15 minutes.
   Serve.

NOTE: Serve with rice or bread preparations.

Mixed Vegetable

½ cauliflower
2 medium-sized potatoes, peeled
¼ lb. pumpkin, peeled
3 long carrots
2 stems broccoli
¼ cup frozen or fresh peas
¼ teaspoon cumin seeds, fennel and kalonji (black onion seeds) mixture or any one of these
1½ teaspoons salt
¾ teaspoon sugar
¼ teaspoon paprika
¼ teaspoon chilli powder
¼ teaspoon turmeric powder
2½ tablespoons oil
2 green chillies (optional)

UTENSIL: one heavy saucepan with a lid.

1. Cut all vegetables into 1″ cubes.
   Wash them.
2. Heat oil.
   Add seed mixture.
   Add all vegetables.
   Add salt, sugar, paprika, chilli and turmeric.
   Fry 5 minutes, stirring well.
3. Reduce heat to low.
   Cover saucepan.
   Simmer for 15 minutes.

Check that vegetables are cooked.
Serve.

NOTE: Vegetables are cooked without any extra water.

Onion Pakoras

2 onions	½ teaspoon chilli powder
7 tablespoons gram powder (besan)	1¼ teaspoons salt
	pinch of baking soda
½ teaspoon kalonji (black onion seeds)	6½ tablespoons water
	oil for deep frying

UTENSILS: one mixing bowl; one frying pan or Indian kerai.

1. Cut onions in thin round pieces, ¼″ thick.
2. Make batter by mixing gram powder, kalonji, chilli, salt, baking soda and water.
   Mix thoroughly.
3. Dip onion pieces in batter, coating them well.
4. Heat oil on high temperature.
   Remove frying pan from cooker and place onion pieces into oil (as many as possible).
5. Reduce heat to medium.
   Place frying pan on the cooker.
6. Fry onion pieces till they are brown all over.
   Serve hot.

NOTE: Onion pakoras go well with drinks as well as at teatime.

Pumpkin Curry

1½ lb. pumpkin	1 teaspoon turmeric powder
2 medium potatoes	1 teaspoon fresh grated ginger or ginger powder
2 onions	
1 teaspoon kalonji or cumin seeds	1 green chilli, cut into pieces (optional)
1½ teaspoons sugar	
1½ teaspoons salt	3 tablespoons vegetable oil
2 bay leaves	¾ cup water

UTENSIL: one saucepan with a lid.

1. Peel vegetables, cut into 1″ cubes and wash.
   Cut onions into thin slices.
2. Heat oil and fry onion for 2–3 minutes.
   Add potato cubes.
   Fry 3–4 minutes.
   Add pumpkin pieces.
3. Add kalonji or cumin seeds.
   Fry for 1 or 2 minutes.
   Add sugar, salt, bay leaves, turmeric and ginger.
   Fry for 4–5 minutes on medium heat.
4. Add water.
   Cover saucepan.
   Cook on medium heat till potatoes are soft.
   Add green chilli pieces.
   Serve.

Pumpkin Chechki

1 lb. pumpkin
¼ teaspoon kalonji (black onion seeds) or cumin seeds
1 green chilli (optional)
½ teaspoon sugar
½ teaspoon salt
2 tablespoons vegetable oil

UTENSIL: one heavy saucepan with a lid.

1. Peel pumpkin and cut into small thin slices (1″ long).
   Wash.
2. Heat oil.
   Add kalonji or cumin seeds and chilli.
   Add pumpkin slices.
   Fry 5 minutes.
3. Reduce heat to low.
   Add salt and sugar.
   Cover saucepan.
   Simmer 10 minutes.

4. Raise heat.
   Fry 5 minutes stirring occasionally.
   Serve.

NOTE: Pumpkin is cooked without any water.

Spinach-Aubergine

½ lb. spinach
1 medium-sized aubergine
1 medium-sized potato
1 bay leaf
½ teaspoon cumin seeds
¼ teaspoon turmeric powder

2 tablespoons vegetable oil
1 teaspoon salt
1 green chilli, cut in half with the seeds washed off (optional)
1 teaspoon ghee (optional)

UTENSILS: one saucepan with a cover or an Indian kerai.

1. Wash spinach under cold tap.
   Slice aubergine into small pieces.
   Peel potato and slice into very small pieces.
2. Heat vegetable oil in the saucepan.
   Add bay leaf and cumin seed. Stir.
   Add potato pieces.
   Fry for 2–3 minutes.
   Add aubergine pieces, spinach, green chilli and turmeric.
   Add salt.
   Cover the saucepan and lower heat to simmer.
3. Cook till potato is done (7–8 minutes).
   Add teaspoon of ghee and serve.

Spinach Fry

5 oz. spinach
1 egg
½ teaspoon salt
¼ teaspoon chilli powder

4 tablespoons flour
4 tablespoons ground rice
oil for frying

UTENSILS: one mixing bowl; one frying pan.

1. Remove stems from spinach.
   Tear spinach leaves into small pieces.
   Wash.
2. Mix spinach leaves, beaten egg, salt, chilli powder, flour and
   ground rice thoroughly.
3. Heat oil in the frying pan.
   Take two tablespoons spinach in hands.
   Shape like a flat ball.
   Fry it in the oil.
   Turn over.
   Fry till both sides are brown.
   You can fry 4 to 5 balls at a time depending on the size of
   the frying pan.
4. Serve hot.

Spring Onion and Potatoes

1 *bunch spring onions*   1 *tablespoon vegetable oil*
2 *medium-sized potatoes*   ½ *teaspoon salt*
¼ *teaspoon cumin seeds*

UTENSILS: one deep frying pan with a cover.

1. Cut spring onion into ½"-long pieces, green included.
   Wash thoroughly.
   Peel potatoes.
   Cut them in thin slices.
2. Heat oil.
   Add cumin seeds.
   Fry for a minute (the aroma will rise but the seeds will not
   get burnt).
   Add spring onions and potatoes.
   Add salt.
   Stir and cover it.
3. Reduce heat to low. Continue cooking, occasionally stirring.

4. Within 10 minutes or so, potatoes will be done.
   Check, and serve hot.

NOTE: This dish goes well with steak (cooked European style).

Stuffed Capsicums

8 *capsicums or green peppers*	1 *teaspoon turmeric powder*
1 *lb. minced meat*	1 *teaspoon cinnamon powder*
3 *small onions, finely sliced*	1½ *teaspoons cumin powder*
3 *cloves garlic, finely sliced*	1 *teaspoon salt*
2 *tablespoons oil*	1 *teaspoon sugar*
1 *tablespoon ghee*	

UTENSILS: one saucepan with a lid. One baking tray covered with foil.

1. Cut tops off capsicums.
   Take out seeds.
   Keep capsicums and tops on one side.
2. Heat oil and ghee together in the saucepan.
   Add garlic.
   Add onion.
   Fry till they are golden brown.
3. Add minced meat.
   Add turmeric, cinnamon, cumin.
   Add salt and sugar.
4. Fry on medium heat for 4–5 minutes
   Cover.
   Cook till juice from meat gets dried up.
5. Fill capsicums with meat and spice mixture.
   Cover them with the tops.
   Place them on the baking tray.
6. Set oven at 300 degrees (Regulo 2).
   Place baking tray in the pre-heated oven.
   Cook for 25 minutes.
   Serve.

Stuffed Tomatoes

8 *large tomatoes*
1 *lb. minced meat*
3 *small onions, finely sliced*
3 *cloves garlic, finely sliced*
2 *tablespoons oil*
1 *tablespoon ghee*

1 *teaspoon turmeric powder*
1 *teaspoon cinnamon powder*
1½ *teaspoons cumin powder*
1 *teaspoon salt*
1 *teaspoon sugar*

UTENSILS: one saucepan with a lid; one baking tray covered with foil.

1. Cut tops off tomatoes.
   Scoop out seeds.
   Keep tomatoes and tops on one side.
2. Heat oil and ghee together in the saucepan.
   Add garlic pieces.
   Add onion pieces.
   Fry till they are golden brown.
3. Add minced meat.
   Add turmeric, cinnamon, cumin.
   Add salt and sugar.
4. Fry on medium heat for 4–5 minutes.
   Cover.
   Cook till juice from meat gets dried up.
5. Fill tomatoes with meat and spice mixture.
   Cover them with the tops.
   Place them on the baking tray.
6. Set oven at 300 degrees (Regulo 2)
   Place baking tray in the pre-heated oven.
   Cook for 25 minutes.
   Serve.

Turnip Curry

3 medium-sized turnips
2 medium-sized potatoes
2 tomatoes
½ cup peas (fresh or frozen)
2 whole cardamoms
½ stick cinnamon, broken into pieces
2 bay leaves
½ teaspoon cumin powder
½ teaspoon paprika powder
¼ teaspoon coriander powder
¼ teaspoon chilli powder (optional)
1 tablespoon yoghourt
1½ teaspoons salt
1 cup water
5 tablespoons oil
1 tablespoon ghee or butter

UTENSIL: one saucepan with a lid.

1. Cut each turnip into 8 pieces.
   Peel potatoes.
   Cut potatoes and tomatoes into small pieces.
2. Boil turnips till they are tender.
   Drain.
3. Heat oil.
   Fry potatoes and turnips together for 5 minutes.
   Add cardamoms, bay leaves and cinnamon.
   Fry for 2 minutes.
4. Add cumin, paprika, coriander, chilli and yoghourt.
   Fry for 2 minutes.
   Add tomatoes.
   Cook on medium heat for 5 minutes.
   Add peas (rinse well if frozen).
5. Add water and salt.
   Bring to boil.
   Cover and cook on medium heat till potatoes are tender.
6. Sprinkle ghee or butter on top.
   Serve.

Vegetable 'Chops'

2 medium-sized potatoes
½ cauliflower
2 carrots
1 cup peas (fresh or frozen)
14 oz. tinned beet (or 2 cups fresh beet, boiled and mashed)
1½ teaspoons salt
1 teaspoon sugar
2 tablespoons sultanas
1 medium-sized onion, finely sliced
1 teaspoon grated ginger
2 green chillies cut into small pieces (optional)
2 tablespoons gram powder (besan) or plain flour
2 eggs
breadcrumbs
oil for deep frying

UTENSILS: one saucepan with lid; one frying pan.

1. Peel potatoes and carrots and cut them into small pieces.
   Cut cauliflower into small pieces.
2. Boil potatoes, carrots, cauliflower and peas till they are tender.
3. Mash and mix together all the boiled vegetables.
   Add canned beets.
   Mash and mix them.
4. Add salt, sugar, sultanas, ginger, onion, flour and chillies to vegetable mixture.
   Mix well.
5. Take one portion of vegetable mixture in your hands.
   Shape it into an oval shape 2″ long and ½″ thick.
   Do the same with the rest of the vegetable mixture.
   You will have approximately 12 'chops'.
6. Cover with breadcrumbs, dip them into beaten egg and then into breadcrumbs again.
7. Heat oil.
   Place as many 'chops' in the oil as you can comfortably.
   Fry on medium heat till they are dark brown on both sides.
   Serve hot.

NOTE: Serve vegetable 'chops' with a rice preparation. Chutney and green salad go well with them. They also go very well with drinks.

Palya Kannada

1 *lb. cabbage*
2 *teaspoons urad dhal*
2 *teaspoons channa dhal*
½ *teaspoon mustard seeds*
4 *whole red chillies*

1 *teaspoon turmeric powder*
2 *teaspoons salt*
5 *tablespoons oil*
1 *tablespoon freshly-grated coconut (optional)*

UTENSIL: one saucepan.

1. Shred cabbage thinly.
2. Heat oil.
   Add mustard seeds. Fry ½ minute.
   Add urad dhal, channa dhal, red chillies. Fry for 2–3 minutes.
   Add cabbage.
   Add turmeric and salt, and coconut if you are using it.
   Stir.
   Cover and cook on low heat.
3. When cabbage is cooked stir.
   Serve hot with rice.

NOTE: Other vegetables like capsicums, beans, ladies' fingers or cauliflower could be substituted for cabbage.

Thoran

3 *cups shredded cabbage*
½ *cup coconut*
4 *green chillies*
2 *cloves garlic*
½ *teaspoon cumin seeds*
½ *teaspoon turmeric powder*

1 *teaspoon salt*
2 *onions, thinly sliced*
½ *teaspoon mustard seeds*
3 *tablespoons ghee*
a little water

UTENSILS: one electric blender; two saucepans.

1. Grind, or blend, coconut, chillies, garlic and cumin seeds together.
   Add turmeric powder.
2. Mix cabbage, paste from step 1, salt and a little water.
   Cover and cook till cabbage is tender and water is dry.

3. Heat ghee.
   Fry onion till lightly brown.
   Add mustard seeds. Fry for a minute.
   Add cabbage mixture.
   Stir well and serve with a variety of rice or bread.

NOTE: If the cabbage is tender and fresh no cooking water is needed. Cover and cook on a low heat.

Moru Kalan

1½ *cups yoghourt*   1 *teaspoon salt*
1½ *cups water*

FOR PASTE:

½ *cup grated coconut*   ½ *teaspoon methe (fenugreek)*
2 *cloves garlic*   *powder*
2 *green chillies*   ½ *teaspoon mustard seeds*
½ *teaspoon turmeric powder* 4 *whole red chillies*
1 *cup of pumpkin, cut into small*   2 *tablespoons ghee*
   pieces, peas, capsicum, cut   2 *tablespoons oil*
   into small pieces

UTENSILS: one electric blender; two saucepans; one earthenware or glass bowl.

1. Make a paste of coconut, garlic, green chillis and turmeric in the blender, using a little water.
2. Mix vegetables and paste from step 2 together with a little water.
   Cook on low heat till vegetables are tender.
3. In the meantime put yoghourt, water and salt in the blender.
   Mix for 2–3 minutes.
   Keep it aside.
4. When vegetables are tender, pour yoghourt from step 3 over them.
   Heat well but do not allow yoghourt to boil.
   Keep it aside.

5. Heat ghee and oil.
   Add mustard seeds.
   Add methe powder and red chillies.
   Fry for 2–3 minutes.
   Add vegetables and yoghourt from step 4.
   Heat well and serve sprinkled with coriander leaves.

NOTE: Moru Kalan is a good side-dish for lunch or dinner. It could be a substitute for soup in a Western menu.

Avial   Mixed Vegetables in Yoghourt

2 medium-sized potatoes
2 medium-sized carrots
1 green cooking banana
2 small capsicums
¼ cup green beans (frozen or fresh)
¼ cup peas (frozen or fresh)
1 teaspoon turmeric powder
2 teaspoons salt

½ cup water
½ cup freshly-grated coconut
2 green chillies
1 teaspoon cumin seeds
1 cup yoghourt
1 tablespoon oil
1 tablespoon coriander leaves or curry leaves

UTENSILS: one medium-sized saucepan; one electric blender.

1. Cut vegetables into thin long pieces. Wash.
2. Cook vegetables with salt, turmeric powder and water on medium heat.
3. Prepare masala (spice).
   Put coconut, cumin seeds and green chillies into blender and make a paste.
4. When vegetables are almost done, add masala paste from step 3.
   Continue to cook for 5 minutes.
5. Beat yoghourt in a cup. Add to vegetables after removing the saucepan from the heat.
6. Pour oil over cooked vegetables.
7. Sprinkle coriander or curry leaves on top.
   Serve with boiled rice.

9

Pulses

❧

Pulses form an essential part of everyday meals in India. Many different varieties are grown – about sixty in all – and they provide the main source of protein for the poorer people. Channa (Gram), Mattar (split peas), Masoor (lentils), Arhar (red lentils), Moong (yellow lentils) – for which recipes are included – are easily available in the West. It is always advisable to wash pulses in running water before cooking.

Dhal

1 *cup gram pulse (channa dhal)*
1 *large cinnamon stick, broken into pieces*
4 *cloves*
4 *whole cardamoms*
4 *bay leaves*
½ *teaspoon turmeric powder*
1 *teaspoon fresh crushed ginger*
or ½ *teaspoon ginger powder*
2 *green chillies (optional)*
1½ *tablespoons sugar*
4 *teaspoons salt*
4 *teaspoons oil*
3 *tablespoons ghee (ordinary butter will do)*
4 *cups water*

UTENSIL: one large saucepan with a lid.

1. Wash gram.
2. Bring water to boil in a large saucepan.
   Add gram and oil.
   Cover it.
   Set temperature at low.

3. When gram is tender (after about an hour and a quarter), add cinnamon stick, cloves, whole cardamoms, bay leaves, turmeric, ginger, sugar and salt.
4. Boil another 20 minutes or so at low temperature.
   Add green chilli and ghee.
   Serve hot.

NOTE: Gram or channa, a high protein food, is available at Indian or Greek grocery stores. This dish could easily be transformed into a delicious soup by increasing the proportion of water, thus making it thinner.

Dhokar Dalna

FOR DHOKA:

1 cup gram pulse (channa dhal) ½ tablespoon salt
2 green chillies, cut into small oil for medium deep frying
  pieces (optional)

FOR CURRY:

2 potatoes, peeled and cut into 2 teaspoons turmeric powder
  small pieces 1 teaspoon paprika powder
1 tomato, cut into small pieces 2 teaspoons salt
2 tablespoons grated ginger 6 tablespoons oil
1½ teaspoons coriander powder 1½ cups water
2 teaspoons cumin powder

UTENSILS: one saucepan; one frying pan; one electric blender.

1. First make Dhoka.
   Wash channa dhal.
   Soak overnight (keep in the refrigerator).
2. Blend channa smooth in the blender using a little water.

3. Mix channa with salt and green chilli pieces.
   Make 18 round balls (like walnuts).
4. Heat oil and fry channa balls till they are dark brown all over.
5. Now make curry.
   Heat oil.
   Add potatoes.
   Fry till they are light brown.
   Add spices, tomatoes and salt.
   Cook 4–5 minutes.
6. Add water.
   Bring to boil.
   Cover and cook on medium heat till potatoes are tender.
7. Add channa balls.
   Cook 8 minutes more.
   Serve.

Dhal Bhatee

½ *cup lentils*　　　　　　　1 *teaspoon salt*
2 *tablespoons butter*　　　　1 *green chilli, cut into pieces*

UTENSIL: one saucepan with a lid.

1. Wash lentils.
   Place in a piece of fine muslin.
   Tie it up.
2. Place it in a saucepan quarter full with cold water.
   Bring to boil.
   Simmer till lentils are tender (approximately half an hour).
3. Place boiled lentils on a plate – mash thoroughly.
   Mix butter, salt and chilli pieces with lentils.
   Serve.

NOTE: You can sprinkle fried onions on top if you like.

Papadom

12 *papadoms** (*broken into*   *oil for frying*
halves)   *available at Indian grocers

UTENSIL: one frying pan.

1. Heat oil on high heat.
   Reduce heat to medium.
   Place one papadom in oil where it will immediately turn crisp.
   Turn it over.
   Place it on kitchen paper.
   Fry the rest.
2. Place in the serving dish.
   Serve hot.

NOTE: Papadoms can be baked slowly over a gas ring or on a charcoal fire.

Lentil Soup

1 *cup lentils*   2 *teaspoons salt*
3½ *cups water*   1 *small onion, sliced*
¼ *teaspoon turmeric powder*   1 *teaspoon grated ginger*
2 *bay leaves*   2 *tablespoons ghee*

UTENSILS: one large saucepan with a lid; one frying pan.

1. Wash lentils in running water 3 or 4 times. Put lentils, water, turmeric and bay leaves in a saucepan.
   Bring to boil.
   Reduce heat to low.
   Cover saucepan and cook for 50 minutes.
   Add salt.
2. Heat ghee in the frying pan.
   Fry onions golden brown.
   Pour over lentils.

Mix thoroughly.
Simmer for 3–4 minutes and serve.

NOTE: This preparation could be served with rice or bread. By increasing the proportion of water it could be transformed into a delicious thin soup.

Split Peas with Vegetables

2 cups split peas
4 cups water
10 radishes
8 medium-sized pieces of pumpkin
½ cauliflower, cut into medium-sized pieces
1 tablespoon grated ginger

4 green chillies (optional)
½ teaspoon turmeric powder
1 teaspoon cumin powder
1 teaspoon sugar
2 teaspoons salt
½ teaspoon cumin seeds
2 tablespoons ghee

UTENSILS: two saucepans with lids.

1. Wash split peas with cold water.
   Mix peas and water.
   Bring to boil.
   Lower heat.
   Simmer for an hour.
2. Add vegetables, ginger, chillies, turmeric, cumin powder, salt and sugar.
   Bring to boil.
   Simmer for 15 minutes.
3. Heat ghee in the saucepan.
   Fry cumin seeds for 1–2 minutes.
   Pour over simmering split peas.
   Serve.

NOTE: Serve with a rice or bread preparation.

Dahibara

1 cup urad dhal (pulse)	2 cups yoghourt
2 teaspoons freshly grated ginger	½ cup water
3 green chillies	½ cup freshly grated coconut
¼ teaspoon hing (asafoetida)	oil for frying
2 teaspoons salt	

UTENSILS: one electric blender; one frying pan; one glass or earthenware bowl.

1. Soak urad dhal in water for 1 hour.
   Grind coarsely in a blender using a little water.
   Add 1 teaspoon ginger, 2 green chillies and hing, and grind together to form a thick paste.
2. Add salt.
   Heat oil in the frying pan.
   Make small balls of urad dhal paste, the size of walnuts.
   Fry them till they are brown.
3. In the meantime put yoghourt, coconut, remaining ginger and chilli and the water in the blender and mix for 2–3 minutes.
   Pour into a bowl and keep it aside.
4. When urad dhal balls are fried, immerse them in yoghourt.
   Let them soak for a few hours.

NOTES:
1. These amounts will make about 20 dahibaras.
2. Keep dahibaras in the refrigerator and serve cold as a side dish for lunch or dinner.

Sambar

1 cup arhar dhal lentils	3 small onions, thinly sliced
1 cup carrots, cut into small pieces	½ cup tamarind
1 cup peas	1½ cups water
	2 teaspoons salt

FOR PASTE:

2 *teaspoons coriander seeds*	2 *whole red chillies*
1 *tablespoon channa dhal*	2 *tablespoons grated coconut*
pinch of methe (fenugreek)	1 *teaspoon mustard seeds*
1 *small cinnamon stick*	4 *tablespoons ghee*

UTENSILS: one pressure cooker; two saucepans.

1. Cook arhar dhal with salt and using water required for lentils (see dhal recipe on page 125) in the pressure cooker for 15 minutes. (Alternatively you can cook it in an ordinary saucepan, though it takes much longer.)
2. Soak tamarind in 1½ cups water.
   Discard tamarind pulp.
   Boil vegetables in tamarind water till tender.
   Keep vegetables and water aside.
3. Heat 2 tablespoons ghee.
   Fry methe and cinnamon for 1 minute.
   Add channa dhal. Fry 2–3 minutes.
   Add coriander seeds, chillies and coconut. Fry for a minute.
   Make into a paste by adding a little water.
4. Now mix together cooked arhar dhal, vegetables and water, and spice paste from step 3.
   Mix well.
5. Heat remaining 2 tablespoons ghee.
   Fry mustard seeds for a minute.
   Add dhal mixture from step 4.
   Now the sambar is ready to be served.

NOTE: Sambar is a well-known dish in South India. Serve it with dosa or idli (see pages 34 and 35).

Rasam Pepperwater

⅓ cup arhar dhal (red lentils)
½ cup dry tamarind
1 teaspoon turmeric powder
2 teaspoons cumin seeds
1 teaspoon peppercorns
2 cloves garlic (optional)
2½ teaspoons salt
3 tablespoons oil

1 teaspoon mustard seeds
3–4 red chillies, broken into pieces
1 teaspoon asafoetida (hing)
½ teaspoon urad dhal
1 tablespoon curry leaves or coriander leaves
3 cups water

UTENSILS: one large saucepan; one pressure cooker; one frying pan.

1. Cook arhar dhal in pressure cooker. Keep on one side.
2. Soak tamarind in 2 cups water for one hour.
   Squeeze out the pulp.
   Strain and keep juice.
3. Fry cumin seeds, peppercorns and chopped garlic for 1 minute.
   Grind them to a paste.
4. Heat oil in saucepan.
   Add mustard seeds, red chillies, asafoetida and urad dhal.
   Fry 2–3 minutes.
   Add tamarind juice and ground spices.
   Add turmeric powder and salt.
   Cook 15 minutes on a low heat. Then add curry leaves.
5. Add arhar dhal.
   Bring to boil and mix well.
   Serve hot.

NOTE: Serve rasam with dosa or idli (pages 34 and 35). It also makes a delicious Western-style soup (though use a little less peppercorn). You can also add small chunks of tomato.

Yellow Lentil Soup

1 cup yellow lentils (moong dhal)	¼ teaspoon chilli powder
3 cups water	½ teaspoon turmeric powder
2 bay leaves	¼ teaspoon cumin seeds
¼ teaspoon cumin powder	1½ teaspoons salt
¼ teaspoon coriander powder	1 teaspoon sugar
	2 tablespoons ghee or butter

UTENSILS: one frying pan, preferably of iron; one medium-sized saucepan with a lid.

1. Fry yellow lentils on a dry frying pan on medium heat for 7–8 minutes stirring constantly.
   Wash them in fresh water.
2. Mix lentils and 3 cups water in the saucepan.
   Bring it to boil.
   Reduce heat to low.
   Cover the saucepan.
3. After ½ hour add cumin powder, coriander, turmeric, chilli.
   Simmer another 15 minutes.
4. Check if lentils are soft.
   Add salt and sugar.
5. Heat ghee in the frying pan.
   Fry cumin seeds and bay leaves gently for 2–3 minutes.
   Pour over simmering lentils.
   Serve hot.

NOTE: This preparation of yellow lentils go well with any pilau dish.

Desserts

※

Since sugar candy and molasses have been known in India from a very early age, it is only natural that a rich cuisine of sweets and desserts should have evolved. Every region has its own specialities, but Bengal leads with its desserts made of chhana and khoya. In this section, I have drawn largely on Bengali sweets and desserts – many of which are now available all over the country.

All the sweets and desserts included in this section can be prepared in advance. Indeed some of them, like rasgullas and pantuas, taste much better if you prepare them in advance. I have included only dishes which are relatively easy to make.

Chamchams

1 *quart milk*
1 *teaspoon semolina*
2 *cups water*

2 *cups sugar*
1 *teaspoon rosewater*

UTENSIL: one large saucepan with a lid.

1. Prepare chhana from 1 quart milk following the recipe on page 19.
   Drain 4 hours.
2. Put chhana on the kitchen top.
   Knead well with the palm of your hand for at least 6 or 7 minutes.
   Mix in the semolina.
   Knead for 2–3 minutes.

Divide chhana into 10 portions.
Shape each portion into a long oval shape pressing lightly.
Each piece should be $\frac{1}{8}''$ thick.
3. Mix water and sugar.
 Bring to boil.
 Put oval-shaped chhana pieces into syrup.
 Cover the saucepan.
4. Boil at medium heat for 35 minutes.
 Put chamchams in a serving dish.
 Pour syrup left in the saucepan over them.
5. Chamchams are served cold.
 Sprinkle rosewater over before serving.

Pongal

$\frac{1}{2}$ *cup moong dhal (yellow lentils)*
$\frac{1}{2}$ *cup Basmati rice*
1 *cup water*
1 *cup milk*
$\frac{1}{2}$ *cup cashew nuts*

2 *tablespoons sultanas*
2 *whole cardamoms, freshly
 ground*
6 *tablespoons brown sugar*
8 *tablespoons ghee*

UTENSIL: one saucepan.

1. Wash moong dhal and rice.
2. Cook dhal and rice together in milk and water.
 Simmer for 10 minutes on low heat.
3. Add sugar, cashew nuts and sultanas and continue to cook.
4. When rice and dhal are soft, add ghee.
5. Cook for altogether $\frac{1}{2}$ hour or so (from step 2 onwards) till rice and dhal are well cooked.
 Sprinkle cardamom powder on the top and serve.

NOTE: This is the traditional dish prepared in the South Indian state of Tamilnadu for the spring festival.

Chhana Jelabi

1 *quart milk for khoya*   2 *cups water*
1 *quart milk for chhana*   *ghee for frying*
1 *teaspoon cake mix*

UTENSILS: one frying pan; one deep serving dish; one saucepan.

1. Make khoya from 1 quart milk following the recipe on page 21.
   Make chhana from 1 quart milk following the recipe on page 19.
2. Mix together chhana and khoya with cake mix.
   Knead well for at least 10 minutes.
3. Take some mixture in hands.
   Roll it into a long strip.
   Then shape it into a flat spiral.
   Make 12 spirals.
4. Heat oil for frying.
   Fry each spiral till it is dark brown on both sides.
5. While frying spirals, make syrup mixing sugar and water.
   Bring it to boil.
   Boil for 5 minutes.
   Keep it warm.
6. Dip jelabis in syrup while still hot.
   Place them in a serving dish.
   Pour syrup over them.
   Serve cold (not refrigerated).

NOTE: Make chhana jelabis the day before you want to serve them. They will then have time to draw in syrup.

Gokul Pitha

1 *quart milk*
3 *tablespoons flour*
1 *teaspoon ghee* }*for batter*
¼ *cup water*

1 *cup sugar*
1 *cup water*
ghee for frying

UTENSILS: one saucepan; one frying pan.

1. Make khoya from 1 quart milk following the recipe on page 21.
   Let it cool.
2. Divide khoya into 12 portions after kneading it 2–3 minutes.
   Shape each portion into a flat round shape.
3. Make a smooth batter, mixing flour with ghee and water.
4. Heat ghee in the frying pan on high heat.
   Remove pan from heat.
   Dip each portion of khoya into batter and place in hot fat.
   You can fry 3 to 4 at one time.
5. Reduce heat to high medium.
   Replace pan on cooker.
   Fry till pithas are golden brown on both sides.
6. Make syrup mixing sugar and water.
   Boil for 5 minutes.
   Place pithas in hot syrup.
7. Keep pithas in syrup for at least 4–5 hours before serving them.

Gajar Halwa   Carrot Halva

1 *lb. carrots*
1 *quart milk*
1 *cup milk*
7½ *tablespoons sugar*

2 *tablespoons sultanas*
½ *tablespoon almonds*
3 *tablespoons ghee*

UTENSILS: one saucepan; one pressure cooker.

1. Peel and cut carrots in small pieces.
   Wash.

2. Cook carrots in pressure cooker with a cup of milk for 3–4 minutes. (Keep heat low.)
   Mash carrots.
3. Bring 1 quart milk to boil.
   Boil on medium heat for $1\frac{1}{2}$ hours.
   Add mashed carrots.
   Mix in sugar, sultanas and ghee.
4. Continue cooking for 25 minutes on medium heat.
   Stir well.
5. Spread halwa on a plate.
   Slice blanched almonds into thin pieces.
   Sprinkle them over halwa.
   Serve cold.

NOTE: You can grate carrots and cook them from the beginning in milk. Thereby you omit step 2.

Kulfi   Ice-Cream with Almonds

2 *cups evaporated milk (or 1*   6 *tablespoons sugar*
  large tin)   1 *teaspoon almond essence*
2 *oz. blanched almonds*

UTENSILS: one electric blender; one mixing bowl; one ice-cream mould.

1. Blend together 2 tablespoons evaporated milk and almonds in an electric blender.
2. Pour contents into the mixing bowl.
   Add the rest of the evaporated milk and sugar.
   Mix thoroughly.
   Add almond essence.
3. Pour into an ice-cream mould.
   Put in the freezing compartment of the refrigerator.
   Ice-cream will be ready within 3 hours.

Labanga Latika   Flour Pastry with Khoya

1 *quart milk*	*tional)*
1 *cup flour*	12 *cloves*
3 *tablespoons ghee*	1 *cup sugar*
2 *pinches baking powder*	½ *cup water*
5 *tablespoons boiling water*	*oil for frying*
1 *teaspoon nutmeg powder (op-*	

UTENSILS: one frying pan; one small saucepan.

1. First make khoya from the milk following the recipe on page 21.
2. Mix flour, ghee and baking powder thoroughly, then add boiling water.
   Divide into 12 portions.
3. Mix khoya with nutmeg powder.
4. Roll out one portion of dough into a thin round shape.
   Put 1 teaspoon khoya in the middle.
   Fold in two sides.
   You now have a rectangle.
   Fold in long ends.
   You now have a square.
   Pin with a clove where folds meet.
   Do the same with each portion of dough.
5. Heat oil in the frying pan.
   Fry labanga latikas till they are light brown.
   Fry them with the clove side downward.
6. Make syrup with sugar and water boiling them 4–5 minutes.
   Immerse each labanga latika in the syrup and place them in the serving dish.
   Serve cold.

Malpoa (method 1)

1½ cups evaporated milk
2 tablespoons Bisquick or any cake mixture
2 tablespoons skimmed milk powder

4 tablespoons plain flour
1½ cups sugar
1½ cups water
ghee for medium deep frying

UTENSILS: earthenware pot or a casserole; one electric blender (optional); one frying pan; one saucepan.

1. Make batter in a pot with evaporated milk, Bisquick, milk powder and flour.
   Put it in the mixer for 2 minutes at medium speed or mix it thoroughly by hand, using a fork or spoon.
2. Make syrup by boiling water and sugar for 5 minutes and keep it hot.
3. Heat oil in the frying pan.
   Pour batter into oil using a large spoon, one spoonful at a time.
   Fry each spoonful of batter till it is golden brown both sides. It is called malpoa.
4. Soak each malpoa when it is fried in the sugary syrup for five minutes.
   Take them out and arrange in a serving dish.
   Pour left-over syrup over malpoas and serve.
5. The above batter will make 12 malpoas.
6. Serve cold. (Do not keep malpoas in refrigerator.)

NOTE: If malpoa breaks when frying, add a little more flour to the batter.

Malpoa (method 2)

1 cup skimmed milk powder
¾ cup milk
2 tablespoons cake mixture
4 tablespoons flour

2 tablespoons sultanas
1½ cups sugar
1½ cups water
¾ cup ghee

UTENSILS: one mixing bowl; one frying pan; one saucepan; one big spoon, preferably round.

1. Make batter with milk powder, milk, cake mixture and flour.
   Add sultanas and 2 tablespoons ghee.
2. Heat ghee in the frying pan.
   Drop in one spoon of batter at a time.
   Cook on medium heat.
   When one side is golden brown, turn it over.
   Go on frying malpoas one by one.
3. While frying malpoas as described in step 2, start making syrup by mixing water and sugar in the saucepan.
   Boil it for 5 minutes.
4. As malpoas are fried, drop them in the hot syrup already prepared.
   Turn them over.
   After soaking each malpoa 10 minutes in syrup, keep them in a deep serving dish to make place for other malpoas.
   You can soak 4 to 5 malpoas at a time depending on the size of the saucepan in which the syrup is.
   When all the malpoas are soaked and arranged in the dish, pour left-over syrup over them.
5. Malpoas are served cold, but never keep them in refrigerator.

NOTE: The above batter will make 10 malpoas or 8, depending on the size of the spoon.

Chhana Malpoa

1 *quart milk for chhana*   3 *tablespoons sultanas*
3 *tablespoons semolina*   1½ *cups sugar* ⎫
3 *tablespoons flour*   1½ *cups water* ⎬ *for syrup*
3 *tablespoons sugar*   *ghee for medium deep frying*
¾ *cup milk (a little less)*

UTENSILS: one mixing bowl; one frying pan; one big spoon, preferably round; one saucepan.

1. Make chhana from the milk following the recipe on page 19. Drain for 2 hours.
2. Make batter with chhana, semolina, flour, sugar and milk.
3. Heat ghee in the frying pan.
   Drop one spoon of batter in at a time.
   Cook on medium heat.
   When one side is golden brown, turn it over.
   Go on frying malpoas one by one.
4. While frying malpoas as described in step 3, start making syrup by mixing water and sugar in the saucepan.
   Boil for 5 minutes.
5. As malpoas are fried, drop them in the hot syrup.
   Turn them over.
   After soaking malpoas 10 minutes in syrup, place them in a deep serving dish to make place for other malpoas in the saucepan.
   When all the malpoas are soaked and arranged in the dish, pour left-over syrup over them.
6. Malpoas are served cold, but never keep them in refrigerator.

NOTE: Above batter will make 10 malpoas depending on the size of the spoon.

Narkel Khoya   Coconut Khoya

1 *quart milk for khoya*	½ *cup milk*
1 *quart milk for chhana*	3 *cardamom seeds*
½ *cup unsweetened dessicated coconut*	4 *tablespoons sugar*

UTENSILS: one small saucepan; one electric blender.

1. Make khoya from 1 quart milk following the recipe on page 21.
   Make chhana from 1 quart milk following the recipe on page 19 and drain 2 hours.
2. Simmer coconut in milk for 10 minutes.

3. Place khoya, chhana and coconut with milk in the blender.
   Add sugar and cardamom.
   Blend for 5 minutes.
4. Place in individual dessert cups and refrigerate.
   Serve cold.

Patisapta

1 *quart milk*
1 *cup semolina*
1½ *cups milk*
¼ *cup (a little less) flour*

3½ *tablespoons sugar*
2 *teaspoons melted ghee*
4 *teaspoons oil*

UTENSILS: one mixing bowl; one heavy frying pan, preferably non-stick.

1. Make khoya from 1 quart milk following the recipe on page 21.
   Add 1 tablespoon sugar to milk while preparing khoya.
2. Soak semolina in 1½ cups milk for 2 hours.
3. Make a batter with the semolina and milk, flour and sugar.
4. Mix oil and ghee together in a cup.
5. Heat frying pan (medium heat).
   Spread a little oil and ghee mixture.
   Pour in 6 dessertspoons of batter.
   Spread it round like a pancake.
   Place 1 tablespoon khoya in the centre of the 'pancake' in a long strip.
   Fold the 'pancake' over.
   Place it in a serving dish.
6. Fry rest of the patisaptas following step 5.
   You will have 12 patisaptas.
7. Refrigerate and serve cold.

NOTE: You can make the batter with ground rice instead of semolina.

Pantuas

2 *cups skimmed milk powder*   *milk for batter*
1 *cup cake mixture*   2 *cups sugar*
$\frac{1}{2}$ *teaspoon baking powder*   3 *cups water*
3 *tablespoons unsalted butter*   *ghee for medium deep frying*

UTENSILS: one mixing bowl; one frying pan; one saucepan.

1. Mix milk powder, cake mixture, baking powder, and butter thoroughly with your hand.
   Crumble the butter and rub it thoroughly into the other ingredients.
   Add enough milk to make a very stiff batter.
2. Take a tablespoon of batter in your hand and shape it into a round ball.
   The above batter will make 17 such round balls.
3. Heat ghee.
   Drop 4 or 5 balls in ghee.
   Reduce heat to low.
   Fry balls for 5–6 minutes till they are golden brown all over.
   Similarly fry the rest of the balls or pantuas.
4. Now mix water and sugar and boil for 5 minutes.
   Turn off the cooker.
   Drop pantuas in still boiling syrup.
   The pantuas will swell drawing in syrup.
5. When cold, place pantuas in a deep serving dish or a casserole and pour syrup over them.
   Serve cold.

NOTE: If you want to serve them for dinner, make the pantuas in the morning. They will have time to draw in syrup and be deliciously soft and sweet. Don't keep them in refrigerator. In India, pantuas are made with chhana (milk cheese) and khoya (milk solidified through evaporation). This is a simplified method.

Payes with Chhana

1 *quart milk*	3 *whole cardamoms*
½ *quart milk for chhana*	⅙ *teaspoon citric acid (sour salt)*
3½ *tablespoons sugar*	2 *tablespoons water*

UTENSIL: one saucepan.

1. Make chhana following the recipe on page 19.
   Drain 4 hours.
2. Bring milk to boil.
   Boil for ½ hour on medium heat.
   Add cardamom seeds
   Boil one hour more.
3. Cube chhana.
   Add chhana pieces to milk.
   Wait till milk starts boiling again.
   Add sugar.
   Wait for boiling to start again.
   Switch off the cooker.
   When the milk completely stops boiling, take the saucepan
   off the cooker and refrigerate.
   Serve cold.

Payes with Rice   Milk Pudding with Rice

1 *quart milk*	3 *tablespoons sugar*
1 *tablespoon Basmati rice*	3 *almonds*

UTENSIL: one medium-sized saucepan.

1. Bring milk to boil on high heat.
   Reduce heat to medium.
   Boil for 30 minutes.
2. Wash rice and add to boiling milk.
   Boil for a further 30 minutes.
3. Add sugar to milk and rice.

4. Blanch almonds and cut them into thin pieces.
   Add to boiling milk and rice.
5. After 5–7 minutes of further boiling, pour in a casserole.
   Put in the refrigerator and serve cold.

Payes with Tangerines

1 *quart milk*	2 *whole cardamoms*
8 *sweet tangerines*	4 *tablespoons sugar*

UTENSIL: one large saucepan.

1. Boil milk on medium heat for $1\frac{1}{2}$ hours.
2. In the meantime, peel tangerines.
   Take one segment in your hands, remove skin and seeds and place the red pulp in a serving dish.
   Do the same with all the others.
   Add 1 tablespoon sugar to tangerine pulp in the serving dish.
3. When milk has boiled for $1\frac{1}{2}$ hours, add 3 tablespoons sugar.
   Wait till it starts boiling again.
   Pour over tangerines in the serving dish.
4. Grind cardamom seeds with a rolling pin or with a pestle and mortar.
   Sprinkle over tangerine and milk mixture.
   Refrigerate.
   Serve cold.

NOTE: You can use tinned tangerines.

Rasgulla (method 1)

1 *quart milk*	2 *cups sugar*
$\frac{1}{2}$ *teaspoon flour*	4 *cups water*
14 *sugar cubes*	1 *teaspoon rosewater*

UTENSILS: one pressure cooker; one glass bowl.

1. Make chhana from 1 quart milk following the recipe on page 19.
   Drain 4 hours.
2. Put chhana on a dry surface.
   Add flour.
   Knead chhana thoroughly with the palm of your hand for at least 5 minutes.
   You will have very smooth white chhana (almost like cream cheese).
   Divide chhana into 14 equal small pieces.
3. Now put sugar and water in the pressure cooker and turn heat up high.
4. Take each portion of chhana into your hand, shape it gently into a ball and put one sugar cube into it.
   Cover the sugar cube and mould back into the original ball shape.
   Go on doing the same with each portion of chhana.
5. When the sugar and water in the pressure cooker start boiling, drop the chhana balls gently one at a time into it.
   Cover the pressure cooker.
   Build up pressure to 15.
6. Cook for exactly 3 minutes.
   Remove the pressure cooker from heat and let it cool at room temperature.
7. Open pressure cooker.
   With a big spoon transfer each rasgulla into a bowl – be gentle or the soft rasgullas will break.
   Pour sugar (syrup) liquid over them.
8. The rasgullas will swell up into round white balls and float in the sugary syrup when they are cold.
9. They keep well in the refrigerator for 3 or 4 days.
   Serve cold rasgullas as a dessert, having sprinkled rosewater over them.

Rasgulla (method 2)

1 *quart milk*   3 *cups water*
1 *level teaspoon semolina*   1 *teaspoon rosewater*
1½ *cups sugar*

UTENSILS: one saucepan with a lid; one potato ricer, if you have one.

1. Prepare chhana from 1 quart milk following the recipe on page 19.
   Drain 4 hours.
2. Put chhana on a table top and knead with the palm of your hand.
   If you have a potato ricer, put chhana through it. It will save effort.
   Then knead for 10 minutes.
   Add semolina.
   Knead for 2–3 minutes.
3. Divide chhana into 12 equal parts.
   Take each portion in your hand, press and mould it into a round ball.
   Do the same with each portion.
4. Put sugar and water in a saucepan.
   Bring it to the boil.
   When syrup is boiling add chhana balls.
   Cover.
   Boil for 30 minutes at medium heat.
   Take off the heat.
5. When cold, take out each rasgulla with a spoon and place in a bowl.
   Pour syrup over rasgullas.
6. Before serving add rosewater.

Rasmalai   Rasgullas in Cream

1 *quart milk*   *4 tablespoons sugar*
½ *pint single cream*   *1 teaspoon rosewater*

UTENSILS: one casserole; one electric blender.

1. Make rasgullas from one quart milk following the recipe
   (method 2) on page 150.
   Cool them.
2. Blend cream and sugar for a moment.
   Pour mixture in a casserole.
   Place rasgullas in it.
3. Add rosewater.
   Refrigerate.
   Serve cold.

Payes with Rasgullas

1 *quart milk for rasgullas*   *3 tablespoons sugar*
1 *quart milk for payes*

UTENSIL: one medium-sized saucepan.

1. Make rasgullas following the recipe on page 150.
2. Bring milk to boil on high heat.
   Reduce heat to medium.
   Boil for one hour.
3. Add sugar.
4. Cut rasgullas into halves.
   Add to boiling milk.
5. Boil 5 minutes more.
   Refrigerate.
   Serve cold.

Payes with Vermicelli

1 *quart milk*
1 *tablespoon vermicelli broken into small pieces*

3½ *tablespoons sugar*
3 *whole cardamoms*

UTENSIL: one large saucepan.

1. Bring milk to boil.
   Add vermicelli.
   Reduce heat to medium.
2. Boil ½ hour.
   Open cardamoms and add them.
3. Boil 1 hour more.
   Add sugar.
   Wait till milk starts boiling again.
   Turn off the cooker.
   Keep milk on the cooker till it completely stops boiling.
   Refrigerate and serve cold.

Payes with Semolina

1 *quart milk*
2 *tablespoons semolina*
2 *whole cardamoms*

3½ *tablespoons sugar*
2 *tablespoons sultanas*
2 *tablespoons ghee*

UTENSILS: one frying pan; one saucepan.

1. Heat ghee in the frying pan.
   Fry semolina till it is dark brown.
   Keep it aside.
2. Bring milk to boil.
   Reduce heat to medium.
3. Boil for ¾ hour.
   Add cardamom seeds, semolina and sultanas.
4. Boil for 20 minutes more.
   Add sugar.

5. After 6–7 minutes of further boiling, pour into a casserole.
   Put in the refrigerator.
   Serve cold.

Rajbhog

2 *quarts milk for chhana*	2 *level teaspoons semolina*
1 *pint milk for khoya*	3 *cups sugar* ⎱ *for syrup*
8 *sultanas or raisins*	5 *cups water* ⎰
2 *pinches of saffron*	2 *teaspoons rosewater*

UTENSIL: one large saucepan with a lid.

1. Make chhana following the recipe on page 19.
   Drain 4 hours.
   Make khoya following the recipe on page 21.
2. Knead chhana well for 5 minutes.
   Add semolina.
   Knead 2 minutes.
   Divide chhana into 8 portions.
3. Take one portion in your hands.
   Shape it into a ball.
   Now make a well or depression in the ball pressing sides up
   with your fingers.
   Put $\frac{1}{4}$ teaspoon khoya, one sultana and a little saffron in the
   well.
   Mould it back into the original shape of a ball, i.e. khoya,
   sultana and saffron are enclosed within the chhana ball.
   Do the same with the rest.
4. Make syrup mixing water and sugar.
   Bring it to boil.
   Drop chhana balls one by one into syrup.
   Cover.
5. Boil for 20 minutes on medium heat.
   Uncover and boil for 15 minutes more.
6. Leave it to cool.

When cold place rajbhogs (chhana balls) into a casserole.
Pour syrup over them.

7. Sprinkle rosewater over the dish before serving.

Sandesh

1 *quart milk*   6 *pistachio nuts*
2 *tablespoons sugar*   2 *whole cardamoms*

UTENSILS: one heavy frying pan or Indian kerai.

1. Prepare chhana from 1 quart milk following the recipe on page 19.
   Drain 4 hours.
2. Place chhana on a dry surface.
   Knead well for 15 minutes.
   Add sugar.
   Knead 5 minutes more.
3. Place chhana in the frying pan.
   Cook on medium heat for 8 minutes stirring continuously with a heavy spoon.
4. Place sandesh on a serving dish.
   Press it down.
   Spread it over the dish.
5. Soak pistachio nuts in water.
   Peel and cut into very thin strips.
   Take cardamom seeds out of shells and grind them on a dry surface with a rolling pin.
   Decorate the top of sandesh with pistachio pieces and ground cardamom.
   Divide sandesh into squares with a knife.
   Serve cold.

Vapa Sandesh

1 *quart milk for chhana*   4 *pistachio nuts cut into thin*
pinch of saffron   *pieces*
3½ *tablespoons sugar*   1 *teaspoon milk*

UTENSILS: one large saucepan; one china plate.

1. Make chhana following the recipe on page 19.
   Drain chhana 4 hours.
2. Soak saffron in 1 teaspoon milk for an hour.
3. Knead chhana for 5 minutes.
   Add milk in which saffron is soaked (keep aside saffron strands).
   Knead 5 minutes more.
   Add sugar.
   Knead 3 or 4 minutes.
4. Fill saucepan three-quarters full of water.
   Bring it to boil.
5. Grease plate with a little ghee or butter.
   Place chhana on the plate.
   Press chhana down, making a round shape, ½″ thick and 5″ in diameter.
6. Place plate over the top of the saucepan.
   Steam for 1 hour and 20 minutes (check whether more water is needed).
   After 10 minutes of steaming, sprinkle pistachio pieces on top of chhana.
7. Let it cool.
   Sprinkle saffron (kept aside) on top.
   Cut into pieces.
   Serve cold.

Sandesh with Ricotta Cheese

1¼ *lb. ricotta cheese*   1¼ *cups evaporated milk*
¼ *lb. unsalted butter*   5 *tablespoons sugar*

UTENSIL: one saucepan.

1. Put butter in the saucepan.
   Heat.
   Let butter melt completely.
   Add cheese.

2. Stir a few times.
   Reduce heat to low.
   Let it boil for 10 minutes stirring occasionally.
3. Add evaporated milk.
   Raise heat to medium.
   Let it boil for 20 minutes.
4. Add sugar.
   Boil for another 20 minutes.
5. Put in a serving dish.
   Refrigerate.
   Serve cold.

Sweet Yoghourt (method 1)

1 *quart milk*   3 *tablespoons sugar*
4 *tablespoons plain yoghourt*

UTENSILS: one saucepan; one casserole with lid.

1. Bring milk to boil.
   Lower heat.
   Go on boiling milk on medium heat for 20 minutes.
   Stir milk occasionally.
2. Add sugar and boil for 10 minutes more.
3. Allow milk to cool at room temperature.
4. When milk feels slightly warm to the touch, add yoghourt.
   Stir thoroughly.
5. Pour mixture into the casserole and cover it.
6. Spread a small thick blanket on a table top.
   Put casserole on the blanket.
   Cover casserole with the blanket and leave it overnight or
   else keep casserole in an airing cupboard overnight.
7. Next morning see whether yoghourt has set.
   If not, set the oven at 300 degrees (Regulo 2) and put the
   casserole into the preheated oven for 8–10 minutes.
8. Put yoghourt into the refrigerator.
   It is taken cold.

NOTES:
1. In the summer, yoghourt will set without any trouble. In the winter you might have to use the oven as described in step 7.
2. It is customary to offer sweet yoghourt alone or along with another sweet dish (made of milk) as dessert.

Sweet Yoghourt (method 2)

1 *large tin (or 2 cups) evaporated*   6 *tablespoons yoghourt*
 milk   8 *tablespoons sugar*

UTENSILS: one pyrex casserole; one egg-beater (hand) or fork.

1. Put 2 oz. of evaporated milk in the casserole and add yoghourt.
 Mix with the fork or egg-beater till the mixture is smooth.
 Never use electric blender or mixer.
2. Pour rest of the evaporated milk over the mixture.
 Add sugar.
 Mix thoroughly.
3. Set oven at 350 degrees (Regulo 4).
 Put in the casserole in the pre-heated oven.
 Keep it there for 20 minutes.
4. Bring out the casserole and put it in the refrigerator.
 Sweet yoghourt is served cold.

11

Snacks

❧

Snacks are very popular in India, especially in the late afternoon and in summer months when the days are long and late suppers are usual. Afternoon tea, or 'tiffin', fits well into this pattern. Every region has its own popular snacks. I have included recipes which are relatively easy to prepare and go well with either tea or drinks at Western homes.

Ghugni with Vegetables

19 oz. tinned chick-peas
½ medium cauliflower
2 medium potatoes
1 medium tomato
2 medium onions, thinly sliced
2 tablespoons grated ginger
2 green chillies (optional) cut into small pieces
1 lemon (juice)
1 teaspoon cumin powder

1 teaspoon turmeric powder
1 teaspoon coriander powder
½ teaspoon cumin seeds
2 whole cardamoms
3 cloves
½ stick cinnamon, broken into pieces
6 tablespoons oil
2 teaspoons salt
¾ cup water

UTENSIL: one saucepan with a lid.

1. Peel potatoes and chop into 8 pieces each.
   Cut tomatoes into 4 pieces.
   Cut cauliflower into medium-sized pieces.
2. Heat oil.
   Fry onions for 4 minutes.
   Add ginger, chilli pieces and tomato.

Fry 2–3 minutes.
Add cauliflower, potatoes, spices and lemon juice.
Cook 5 minutes.
3. Add water and salt.
Bring to boil.
Cover and cook on medium heat till potatoes are tender.
4. Add chick-peas.
Cook 10 minutes more.
Serve.

Ghugni with Meat

1 *lb. minced meat*	2 *teaspoons turmeric powder*
19 *oz. tinned chick-peas*	½ *teaspoon cumin seeds*
2 *medium potatoes*	2 *whole cardamoms*
1 *medium tomato*	6 *cloves*
2 *medium onions, thinly sliced*	½ *stick cinnamon, broken into*
2 *tablespoons grated ginger*	*pieces*
2 *green chillies (optional), cut*	1½ *teaspoons coriander powder*
into small pieces	8 *tablespoons oil*
1 *lemon (juice)*	4 *teaspoons salt*
2 *teaspoons cumin powder*	1 *cup water*

UTENSIL: one saucepan with a lid.

1. Cut each potato into 8 pieces.
Cut tomato into 4 pieces.
2. Heat oil.
Fry onions for 4 minutes.
Add ginger, chilli pieces and tomato.
Fry 2–3 minutes.
Add minced meat and lemon juice.
Add potatoes and spices.
Cook 5 minutes.
3. Add water and salt.
Bring to boil.
Cover and cook on medium heat till potatoes are tender.

4. Add chick-peas.
   Cook 10 minutes more.
   Serve.

Dahi Goja

1½ cups flour
3 tablespoons ghee
4 heaped tablespoons yoghourt
1 cup sugar } *for syrup*
¼ cup water }
ghee for frying

UTENSILS: one frying pan or Indian kerai; one saucepan.

1. Mix flour and ghee well.
   Add yoghourt.
   Make a dough.
   Knead well.
   (Do not use any water.)
2. Divide dough into 16 portions.
   Take one portion.
   Shape it into a ball.
   Roll it out in a flat round shape, about as thick as a normal pie crust.
   Frill the edges with your fingers.
3. Heat ghee in frying pan.
   Fry gojas one at a time on medium heat till they are dark brown on both sides.
   When you are frying a goja, put a little pressure in the middle with a spoon.
4. Make syrup, mixing sugar and water.
   Bring it to boil.
   Boil for 2–3 minutes.
5. Dip gojas into hot syrup and then place it on a plate to drain off excess syrup.
   Soak and drain all the gojas.
6. When gojas are cold, store them in an airtight tin.
   They will keep for a few days.

Khasta Goja

1 *cup flour*
½ *cup Bisquick or any cake mixture*
pinch of baking soda
¼ *cup (a little more) water*

3 *tablespoons ghee*
1 *cup sugar* ⎱
¼ *cup water* ⎰ *for syrup*
ghee for medium deep frying

UTENSILS: one mixing bowl; one small saucepan; one frying pan or Indian kerai.

1. Mix flour, cake mixture, baking soda and 3 tablespoons ghee.
   Add water.
   Knead dough well for a few minutes.
2. Divide dough in half.
   Take one portion in your hands.
   Shape it into a ball.
   Roll out to 1″ thickness 4 or 5 times.
   Make vertical cuts, 1″ apart.
   Make horizontal cuts, 1″ apart.
   You now have 1″ cubes.
   Do the same with the other portion.
3. Heat ghee in the frying pan.
   Place 7 or 8 cubes in ghee.
   Fry on low heat till they are dark brown on both sides (they will swell up).
   Fry the rest.
4. Prepare syrup by mixing sugar and water.
   Boil for 2–3 minutes.
5. Place fried gojas in syrup.
   Stir continuously on high heat till syrup gets dried up.
   It should stick to the gojas.
   Place them on a plate.
   When cold keep in a tin or box.

NOTE: Gojas will keep for a few days in an airtight tin.

Kucho Goja

1 *cup flour* $\frac{3}{4}$ *cup sugar* ⎱
1$\frac{1}{2}$ *tablespoons ghee* $\frac{1}{3}$ *cup water* ⎰ *for syrup*
$\frac{1}{4}$ *cup (and a little more) water*   *ghee for medium deep-frying*

UTENSILS: one mixing bowl; one deep frying pan or Indian kerai; one saucepan.

1. Mix flour with ghee.
   Add water.
   Make a dough and knead well.
2. Divide dough into three portions.
   Roll out one portion thinly.
3. Make horizontal cuts $\frac{1}{2}''$ apart on the rolled out dough, followed by vertical cuts, $\frac{1}{2}''$ apart.
   You now have small cubes.
   Do the same with the other portions.
4. Heat ghee in the frying pan.
   Fry flour cubes till they are darkish brown on both sides.
5. Mix sugar and water in the saucepan.
   Boil for 4 minutes on medium heat.
6. Place fried cubes into syrup and stir.
   Place in a serving dish.
   Serve cold.

NOTE: Gojas will keep for a few days in an airtight tin.

Nonta Halwa   Salted Halva

1 *cup semolina*   *into small pieces*
1 *medium-sized onion, cut into*   3 *tablespoons vegetable oil*
   small pieces   1 *teaspoon salt*
1 *teaspoon finely-sliced ginger*   3 *cups water*
2 *green chillies (optional), cut*

UTENSIL: one Indian kerai or saucepan.

1. Heat oil in the saucepan.
   Fry onion for 2–3 minutes.
   Add ginger.
   Add semolina.
   Add chillies.
   Fry for 5 minutes stirring constantly.
   Add water.
   Bring to boil.
   Add salt.
2. Reduce heat to low.
   Cook 7–8 minutes more.
   Serve.

Misti Halwa   Sweet Halva

1 *cup semolina*	2 *tablespoons raisins or sultanas*
8 *tablespoons ghee*	4 *almonds, finely cut*
1 *cup sugar*	3 *cups of water*

UTENSIL: one Indian kerai or one saucepan.

1. Heat ghee in the saucepan.
   Fry semolina brown.
2. Add water and sugar.
   Add raisins and almonds.
3. Let it boil till it thickens (approximately 5–7 minutes).
   Stir occasionally.
   Serve.

Fish Kachuris   Flour Pastry Stuffed with Fish

1 *lb. fish fillet*	$\frac{1}{2}$ *teaspoon salt*
1 *medium onion, grated*	1 *teaspoon sugar*
$1\frac{1}{2}$ *teaspoons grated ginger*	$\frac{1}{4}$ *cup vegetable oil*

FOR DOUGH:

2 *cups flour*
2 *tablespoons ghee*
1 *teaspoon salt*

$\frac{1}{2}$ *cup water* (*approximately*)
$\frac{3}{4}$ *cup ghee for frying* (*or any vegetable oil will do*)

UTENSILS: one saucepan; one deep frying pan or Indian kerai.

1. Boil fish for 5 minutes. Mash it.
2. Heat oil.
   Fry grated onion for 2–3 minutes.
   Add mashed fish.
   Add ginger, sugar and salt.
   Go on, on medium heat frying for 15 minutes.
   Keep it aside.
3. Make a very stiff dough with flour, salt, ghee and water.
   Knead well.
   Divide dough into 18 equal parts.
   Take one portion of dough in your hand. Shape it into a ball.
   Then make a deep well or depression inside the ball.
   Put fish stuffing into this well and bring sides of dough shell or ball together over the stuffing and enclose it in dough casing.
   Do the same with each portion of dough. You now have 18 kachuris.
4. Roll out each kachuri in a round shape, make it thin but not so thin as to break dough casing.
5. Heat ghee in a frying pan.
   Fry each kachuri in hot ghee.
   While frying put a little pressure in the middle of kachuri with a frying spoon, kanchuri will swell up. Turn it over.
   Fry for $\frac{1}{2}$ minute – kachuris should be light brown on both sides.
   Fry all of them.
   Serve hot.

Pea Kachuris   Flour Pastry Stuffed with Peas

¾ *lb. peas (frozen or fresh)*	*1 teaspoon sugar*
1 teaspoon cumin seeds	*½ teaspoon salt*
1 teaspoon ginger powder	*4 tablespoons oil*

FOR DOUGH:

2 cups flour	*½ cup (and a little more) water*
½ teaspoon salt	*¾ cup ghee for frying (any vege-*
2 tablespoons ghee	*table oil will do)*

UTENSILS: one electric blender; one saucepan; one deep frying pan.

1. Wash frozen peas in hot water from the tap.
   Put them in an electric blender to make a pulp.
2. Fry cumin seeds in a dry frying pan for 2 minutes till you can smell the aroma.
   Place them on a dry surface and grind with a rolling pin.
   If you find this process too difficult you might use ready-ground cumin powder.
3. Heat oil.
   Add blended peas.
   Lower heat from high to medium.
   Go on frying for 10 minutes.
   Add salt, sugar and ginger powder.
   Fry on for another 5 minutes, add ground cumin seed.
   Fry a little more – 3–4 minutes.
   Take it off the cooker and keep aside.
4. Make a very stiff dough with flour, salt, 2 tablespoons ghee and water.
   Knead well with your hands.
   Divide dough into 18 equal parts.
   Take one portion of dough in your hand. Shape it into a ball.
   Then make a deep well or depression inside the ball.
   Put peas stuffing into the well and bring sides of dough shell

or ball together over the stuffing and enclose it in dough casing.

Do the same with each portion of dough.

You now have 18 kachuris.

5. Roll out each kachuri in a round shape, make it thin but not so thin as to break dough casing.

6. Heat ghee in frying pan.

Fry each kachuri in hot ghee.

While frying put a little pressure in the middle of kachuri with a frying spoon, kachuri will swell up.

Turn it over.

Fry for ½ minute – each kachuri should be light brown on both sides.

Fry all of them.

Serve hot.

NOTE: Kachuris are delicious at teatime or served as a savoury with drinks. They could also be served instead of rice or bread at supper.

Nimkis

1 *cup flour*
¼ *teaspoon salt*
¼ *teaspoon kalonji (black onion seeds)*
3 *tablespoons ghee*

pinch of baking soda
drop of lemon juice
¼ *cup (and a little more) water*
ghee or oil for deep frying

UTENSILS: one mixing bowl; one frying pan or Indian kerai.

1. Mix flour with salt, kalonji, baking soda and lemon juice.
Add 3 tablespoons ghee.
Mix thoroughly.
Add water.
Knead well for 10 minutes.

2. Divide dough into 10 equal portions.
Roll out one portion to make a thin round shape.

Fold twice to make a triangle.
Do the same with the rest.
3. Heat oil for deep frying. Fry nimkis till they are golden brown on both sides.
You can fry 3 to 4 nimkis at a time depending on the size of your frying pan.

Kucho Nimkis

1 *cup flour*
2 *tablespoons ghee*
½ *level teaspoon salt*
a pinch of baking soda

a few drops of lemon juice
¼ *cup (a little less) water*
ghee for medium deep frying

UTENSILS: one mixing bowl; one frying pan or Indian kerai.

1. Mix flour with ghee, salt, baking soda, lemon juice.
Mix thoroughly.
Add water.
Make a dough and knead well.
2. Divide dough into three portions.
Roll out one portion to ½″ thickness.
3. Make horizontal cuts ½″ apart on the rolled-out dough, followed by vertical cuts, ½″ apart.
You have now small ½″ cubes.
Do the same with the rest.
4. Fry them in hot ghee till they are darkish brown.
Serve hot or cold.

NOTE: You can preserve kucho nimkis in airtight tins for a few days.

Cauliflower Samosas

FOR STUFFING:

1 *medium-sized cauliflower*   1 *teaspoon salt*
⅔ *cup peas (frozen or fresh)*   2 *teaspoons sugar*
3 *tablespoons sultanas*   3 *tablespoons oil*
2 *teaspoons cumin seeds*

FOR DOUGH:

1½ *cups plain flour*   4 *tablespoons ghee*
¼ *teaspoon salt*   ¼ *cup (a little more) water*
pinch of baking powder   *ghee or oil for deep frying*

UTENSILS: one mixing bowl; one saucepan; one frying pan or
Indian kerai.

1. Cut cauliflower into very small pieces.
   Wash. Wash frozen peas in warm water.
2. Heat frying pan.
   Fry cumin seeds dry for ½ minute till you can smell the aroma.
   Place cumin seeds on a dry surface.
   Crush with a rolling pin.
3. Heat oil in the saucepan.
   Place cauliflower pieces in the oil.
   Fry 2–3 minutes.
   Add peas, sultanas, salt and sugar.
   Cover.
   Simmer till cauliflower is tender.
   Raise heat to dry it completely.
   Add cumin seed powder.
   Keep it aside.
4. Make dough mixing flour, salt, baking powder, 4 table-
   spoons ghee, followed by water.
   Knead well.
5. Divide dough into 9 portions.
   Knead well.

Take one portion in your hands, shape into a ball, roll it out
as thin and round as possible using a little dry flour.
Cut it in half.
Take one semicircle in your hands.
Close together the edges of the side which has been cut with
a little water.
You now have a cone in your hands.
Place cauliflower stuffing inside the cone.
Using a little water close the open edges tightly.
You now have a three-cornered samosa stuffed with cauli-
flower.
Continue the same process with the rest.
You now have 18 samosas.
6. Heat oil in the frying pan on high heat.
Remove pan from the cooker and place 3 or 4 samosas in oil.
Lower heat to medium.
Fry samosas till they are brown all over.
Serve hot.

Meat Samosas

FOR STUFFING:

1 *lb. minced meat*	1 *tablespoon oil*
½ *cup water*	2 *tablespoons ghee*
1½ *teaspoons salt*	3 *onions, thinly sliced*
¼ *teaspoon turmeric powder*	¼ *teaspoon chilli powder*
1½ *teaspoons freshly ground*	1½ *tablespoons sultanas*
cumin seeds	2 *teaspoons sugar*

FOR DOUGH:

1½ *cups flour*	¼ *cup (a little more) water*
¼ *teaspoon salt*	*ghee or oil for medium deep-*
pinch of baking powder	*frying*
4 *tablespoons ghee*	

UTENSILS: one mixing bowl; one saucepan; one frying pan
or Indian kerai.

1. Mix minced meat, salt, turmeric and water in a saucepan.
   Boil till meat is tender.
   Drain.
2. Heat frying pan without any oil.
   Roast cumin seeds on it for 1–2 minutes till you can smell the aroma.
   Place cumin seeds on a dry surface.
   Crush with a rolling pin.
3. Heat oil and ghee together.
   Fry onion pieces till they are golden brown.
   Add boiled minced meat, chilli powder, sultanas and sugar.
   Fry for 5 minutes.
   Add cumin seed powder.
   Fry for 2 minutes.
   Keep it aside.
4. Make dough by mixing flour, salt, baking powder and ghee, followed by water.
   Knead well.
5. Divide dough into 9 portions.
   Take one portion, shape into a ball, roll it out as thin and round as possible using a little dry flour.
   Cut it in half.
   Take one semi-circle in your hands.
   Close together the edges of the cut side with a little water.
   You now have a cone in your hands.
   Place minced meat stuffing inside the cone.
   Using a little water close the open edges tightly.
   You now have a three-cornered samosa stuffed with minced meat.
   Continue the same process with the rest.
   You now have 18 samosas.
6. Heat oil in the frying pan on high heat.
   Remove pan from the cooker and place 3 or 4 samosas in oil.
   Lower heat to medium.
   Fry samosas till they are golden brown all over.
   Serve hot.

12

Salads, Chutney, Sherbet

Out of the wide number of recipes used in India I have selected only those which can be made easily in England. For instance, I have excluded all those pickles which have to be left standing in the sun for the best results. Again, green mangoes are not easily available in either England or North America. This means I have had to exclude a wide range of delicious chutneys, pickles and sherbets from my list. The recipes in this section have all been prepared by me in England and North America using locally available ingredients.

Raita   Cucumber Salad

2 medium cucumbers	*1½ tablespoons milk*
1 teaspoon salt	*1 teaspoon cumin seeds*
3 tablespoons sour cream	

UTENSILS: one earthenware or glass bowl; one frying pan.

1. Peel cucumbers.
   Discard seeds.
   Grate the flesh.
   Mix grated cucumber and salt.
   Water will come out.
   Squeeze out water.
2. Mix sour cream, milk and cucumber.
3. Fry cumin seeds on a dry frying pan for 2–3 minutes till you can smell the aroma.

Crush them with a rolling pin on a dry surface.
Mix with cucumber, sour cream and milk mixture.

NOTE: Raita is delicious with any meat or pilau dish including
Biryani.

Tomato with Sour Cream

1 *large tomato*
3 *tablespoons sour cream*
1½ *tablespoons milk*

½ *teaspoon salt*
1 *teaspoon cumin seeds*

UTENSILS: one earthenware or glass bowl; one frying pan.

1. Cut tomato into very thin small pieces.
2. Mix sour cream, milk and salt.
   Add tomato pieces.
3. Fry cumin seeds on a dry frying pan for 2–3 minutes till you
   can smell the aroma.
   Crush them with a rolling pin on a dry surface.
   Mix with tomato, sour cream and milk mixture.
4. Serve cold.

NOTE: This salad goes well with any meat or pilau dish.

Tomato-Onion

2 *large red tomatoes*
1 *small onion*
2 *tablespoons white vinegar*

a pinch of salt
a pinch of pepper
½ *teaspoon lemon juice*

UTENSIL: one earthenware or glass bowl.

1. Slice tomatoes into thin small pieces.
   Slice onion very finely.
2. Put onion, tomato, vinegar, salt, pepper and lemon juice in
   the bowl.
   Mix thoroughly.
   Put it in the refrigerator.

3. Make this salad at least 2 or 3 hours before serving.

NOTE: This salad goes well with meat dishes, particularly with minced meat 'chops'.

Apple Chutney

2 green apples
¼ teaspoon mustard seeds
½ teaspoon salt
2 tablespoons sugar

½ lemon (juice)
1 tablespoon oil
½ cup water
1 clove garlic, coarsely chopped

UTENSIL: one saucepan with a lid.

1. Cut apples into long thick pieces.
   Take out the cores.
2. Heat oil in the saucepan.
   Add mustard seeds.
   Fry 1 minute.
   Add apple pieces, salt, sugar, lemon juice.
   Cook for 2–3 minutes.
3. Pour in water.
   Cover.
   Simmer for 8 minutes, or till apple is really soft.
4. Remove from cooker.
   Add garlic pieces and stir.
   Cover.
   Keep for ½ hour.
   Take out the garlic pieces and refrigerate the apple chutney.
   Serve cold.

Coconut Chutney

¾ cup dessicated, unsweetened coconut
1 cup boiling water
½ teaspoon sugar
1 teaspoon salt

1 teaspoon finely grated ginger (or crushed ginger)
1 green chilli (optional) cut into small pieces
¼ lemon (juice)

UTENSILS: one glass or earthenware bowl; one electric blender.

1. Pour boiling water over coconut.
   Leave it for 2 hours.
2. Place coconut and water in the blender.
   Add ginger, salt and sugar.
   Blend a little.
3. Pour in the bowl.
   Add chilli pieces and lemon juice.
   Serve cold.

NOTE: Serve with meat dishes, particularly kebabs, 'chops' and pakoras, and with bread.

Pudina Chutney   Mint Chutney

1 *cup mint leaves*
1 *clove, garlic, chopped*
1 *green chilli, cut into pieces* or
  ¼ *teaspoon chilli powder*
2 *teaspoons ground mango* or 1

tablespoon lemon juice
1 *teaspoon salt*
1 *teaspoon sugar*
1 *tablespoon oil*

UTENSILS: one electric blender; one glass bowl.

1. Wash mint under running water.
2. Place mint, garlic, chilli, ground mango or lemon juice, salt, sugar and oil in the blender.
   Blend for a few minutes.
3. Transfer to a glass dish and serve.

Dhania Chutney   Coriander Chutney

The method for coriander chutney is the same as for mint chutney, except that coriander is substituted for mint.

Prune Chutney

1 *cup prunes*	1 *teaspoon cumin seeds*
½ *cup sultanas*	¼ *teaspoon salt*
1 *tablespoon dry tamarind (imli)*	1½ *cups water*
1 *tablespoon vegetable oil*	2 *tablespoons sugar*

UTENSILS: one saucepan; one glass or earthenware bowl; one frying pan, preferably iron.

1. Soak prunes and sultanas in water (to be discarded later) for at least 2 hours.
   Soak tamarind pieces with 1½ cups water in a bowl.
2. Crush soaked tamarind pieces in the water in which it has been soaked.
   Throw away tamarind pulp and keep the liquid.
3. Heat vegetable oil.
   Add prunes and sultanas (having discarded water).
   Add sugar and salt.
   Add tamarind water.
   Bring it to boil.
   Continue cooking on medium to high heat.
4. Roast cumin seeds for 2–3 minutes on a dry pan (preferably iron one).
   Grind them on a dry surface with a rolling pin.
5. When prunes are soft, pour the mixture in the bowl and sprinkle cumin seed powder on top.
   Keep in the refrigerator.

NOTE: This chutney goes well with any meat dish.

Pineapple Chutney

19 *oz. tinned pineapple* or 1½ *cups fresh pineapple, finely chopped*	1 *whole red chilli (optional)*
	1 *tablespoon oil*
3 *tablespoons unsweetened coconut (dessicated or freshly grated)*	¼ *teaspoon mustard seeds*
	¼ *teaspoon salt*
	1 *cup water*

UTENSIL: one saucepan with a lid.

1. Drain pineapple pieces, if tinned.
2. Heat oil in the saucepan.
   Add mustard seeds.
   Fry for a minute.
   Add pineapple pieces, salt and coconut.
   Fry for a minute.
3. Discard seeds in red chilli.
   Break it into pieces.
   Add them to pineapple mixture.
4. Add water.
   Bring to boil.
   Simmer for 10 minutes.
   Refrigerate.
   Serve cold.

Pineapple and Tomato Chutney

19 oz. tinned pineapple cubes or
  1½ cups fresh pineapple, finely
  chopped
2 tomatoes, cut into small pieces
2 tablespoons oil
¼ teaspoon mustard seeds

¼ teaspoon turmeric powder
¼ teaspoon salt
1 tablespoon sugar
2 tablespoons sultanas
¼ cup water

UTENSIL: one saucepan with a lid.

1. Heat oil.
   Add mustard seeds.
   Fry 1 minute.
   Add tomato and pineapple pieces.
   Add turmeric, salt, sugar and sultanas.
   Fry 2–3 minutes on medium heat.
2. Add water.
   Bring to boil.

Simmer for 15 minutes.
Refrigerate.

NOTE: This chutney goes well with pilau and meat dishes.

Tomato Chutney

5 medium tomatoes, cut into pieces
½ teaspoon freshly grated ginger
2 tablespoons sultanas
2 tablespoons sugar
½ teaspoon salt

1 red chilli, minus its seeds, cut into pieces (optional)
1 teaspoon cumin seeds
1 tablespoon vegetable oil or ghee
¼ cup water

UTENSILS: one saucepan; one frying pan, preferably an iron one; one glass or earthenware bowl.

1. Heat oil in saucepan.
   Add tomatoes, ginger, sultanas, sugar, salt and chilli.
   Add water.
   Bring to boil.
2. Cover and let tomatoes boil at medium heat.
3. Meanwhile roast cumin seeds dry on the frying pan (do not use any fat) until you can smell the aroma.
   Remove from heat.
   Transfer cumin seeds to a dry surface or a mortar and crush.
4. When tomatoes have thickened, making a thick purée, add powdered cumin seed.
   Pour mixture into a glass, or earthenware bowl, and set aside to cool.
   When cold, put into the refrigerator (bottom shelf).

NOTE: This chutney goes well with meat and rice. It keeps for 2 or 3 days. But never keep it in any metal pot, such as copper or aluminium.

Gholer Sherbet

1 *cup plain yoghourt*   1 *tablespoon sugar*
½ *cup water*   2 *teaspoons rosewater*

UTENSIL: one electric blender.

1. Place yoghourt, water and sugar in the blender.
   Blend for a minute.
2. Add rosewater.
   Serve chilled as a refreshing drink.

NOTE: You can also make sherbet with fruit-flavoured yoghourt, in which case do not add rosewater. Serve chilled yoghourt sherbet on a hot day.

Watermelon Sherbet

3 *lb. watermelon*   3 *tablespoons sugar*
3½ *tablespoons yoghourt*

UTENSIL: one electric blender.

1. Peel the watermelon.
   Cut it into chunks.
   Throw away all seeds.
2. Place watermelon pieces in the blender.
   Add yoghourt and sugar.
   Blend for a moment.
   Refrigerate.
   Serve cold, in glasses.

Index